doug fields

help
I'm a student leader
practical ideas and guidance on leadership

doug fields

help

I'm a student leader
practical ideas and guidance on leadership

ZONDERVAN®

Youth Specialties
.com

ZONDERVAN.com/
AUTHORTRACKER
follow your favorite authors

Help! I'm a student leader!: practical ideas and guidance on leadership
Copyright © 2005 by Doug Fields

Youth Specialties Products, 300 South Pierce Street, El Cajon, CA 92020, are published
by Zondervan, 5300 Patterson Avenue SE, Grand Rapids, MI 49530

Library of Congress Cataloging-in-Publication Data

Fields, Doug, 1962–
  Help! I'm a student leader! : practical ideas and guidance on leadership / by Doug
Fields.
    p. cm.
  ISBN-10: 0-310-25961-4 (pbk.)
  ISBN-13: 978-0-310-25961-9 (pbk.)
  1. Church work with teenagers. 2. Church youth workers. 3. Christian leadership. I.
Title.

  BV4447.F54 2005
  259'.23—dc22

                                                                              2004030559

Unless otherwise indicated, all Scripture quotations are taken from the Holy Bible: New
International Version (North American Edition). Copyright © 1973, 1978, 1984 by International Bible Society. Used by permission of Zondervan.

Some of the anecdotal illustrations in this book are true to life and are included with the
permission of the persons involved. All other illustrations are composites of real situations, and any resemblance to people living or dead is coincidental.

Web site addresses listed in this book were current at the time of publication. Please contact Youth Specialties via e-mail (YS@YouthSpecialties.com) to report URLs that are no
longer operational and replacement URLs if available.

Editorial direction by Dave Urbanski
Editing by Ivy Beckwith
Proofreading by Kristi Robison and Janie Wilkerson
Interior Design by SharpSeven Design
Cover Design by Holly Sharp
Printed in the United States of America

06 07 08 09 10 • 14 13 12 11 10 9 8 7 6

This book is dedicated to my youth pastor, Jim Burns.

Thank you, Jim, for believing in me when I was a teenager, asking me to become a leader, and being the first person to give me an opportunity to serve God with my gifts. I am forever grateful. I love you!

I also want to thank the many friends who helped me put this book together: Dennis Beckner was a huge help in many different ways; Matt McGill once again read every word and continues to help me influence others through the written word; thanks also to Linda Kaye and the rest of the crew at Simply Youth Ministry. The student leaders from Saddleback Church who read the manuscript and offered input were Michael Rosenbaum, Tom Hester, Sara Mimbs, Laura Alden, Rachel Gochenour, Curtis Hill, and Alyssa Holladay—I'm so thankful for your ministry at Saddleback. (Alyssa, I'm so proud of you for making your extended contribution to this project.) I wish I could list every student leader I've worked with and loved over the last 25 years—it's been so much fun to watch you deepen your love for Jesus and pursue ministry. Finally, to my cool, supportive, fun family: Cathy, I love being your husband! Torie, Cody and Cassie—I love being called "dad" and watching you grow into leaders as well.

TABLE OF CONTENTS

INTRODUCTION - Read This First!

Let me begin with a promise—if you read this book cover to cover, think about what you've read, and discuss the principles with other leaders, I promise you'll never be the same.

The book you're holding is filled with leadership tips and ideas helpful to your growth as a student leader. I've watched amazing life changes happen to students who didn't think they were leaders or who didn't understand Christian leadership—these students transformed into unbelievable leaders for God. If you're ready to discover more about being a student leader, then dig in, open up your heart, and prepare for God to do something great in your life.

I wish I had a book like this when I was a teenager! Like you I was a student leader in my youth ministry. If any books on student leadership existed, I didn't know about them. Actually, I didn't even know what it meant to be considered a leader. I was fortunate enough to have a youth pastor who believed in me and saw something in me I didn't see in myself. When I was in ninth grade, he said, "Doug, I want you to go on a leadership retreat because I think you have something to offer others, and I want to prepare you for ministry." Honestly, I had no idea what he was talking about, but I really liked him, so I said yes. (It's funny now, but my first act as a leader was to convince him to pay my expenses for the retreat. He agreed. I went. My life was changed, and I've never been the same. I guess I should pay him back now.)

I want to take you on a leadership retreat through the pages of this book. I hope someone paid for your trip (bought you this book), and I hope you'll commit to journey with me as I try to teach you what I've learned and taught thousands of students in more than 25 years of being a youth pastor. I wrote this book especially for the student leaders in my church because I love them and want to watch them continue to grow. Please read this as if you are a student in my youth group—a student I care about, someone I want to see mature in faith, a student leader who will impact the world for Jesus Christ, and someone who God wants to use to serve and honor him.

Are you ready for this leadership trip?

☐ *yes*   ☐ *no*

Do you consider yourself a student leader?
☐ *yes*   ☐ *no*

If either answer is no, what will it take for you to prepare for the journey and consider yourself a student leader? Think about that for a minute. If you see yourself having little potential as a leader, you'll be tempted to skim this book and move on without considering how these ideas, actions, and challenges could impact you and those around you.

The truth is, you have the leadership potential I'm talking about if...

1. You have a relationship with God.
2. You have a heart and mind open to learning and growing.
3. You want to help others.
4. You can handle being challenged.
5. You want your life to count for something.

Almost immediately you'll find out that leadership isn't about popularity. It's not about charisma, and it doesn't require you to speak in front of others. If you want to serve God and have a heart that gets excited about helping others, then you've got what it takes to be a leader.

Now does that describe you?

☐ *yes*   ☐ *no*

If you answered yes, I'm so excited to help you and challenge you!

Before you begin chapter one

Take a few moments to write down your current definition of *student leadership*. Don't worry about having a *right* answer—for the moment there is no correct answer. I'm asking you to do this because when you finish the book, I'll ask you to rewrite a definition of *student leadership* based on what you've learned. Then you'll compare the two definitions to see if you've learned anything and if our leadership retreat was worth your time.

I think it will be. I'm grateful to God for teenagers like you who want to make a difference with their lives. I hope to meet you someday and hear about how God is using you!

Blessings,

Doug Fields

Alyssa's Notes

At the end of each chapter you'll find a short summary including comments from Alyssa, a student in my ministry whom I asked to add her thoughts to each chapter. I think she's really sharp, caring, a lover of Jesus, and an outstanding student leader. You'll enjoy reading her summaries, and you'll see into the heart of a peer who is trying to follow Jesus, survive school, serve in a youth group, care for her family, and be a leader. I believe one day you'll be hearing her name, listening to her speak, or reading her books. She's a normal teenager like you who is serving God in great ways.

My Definitions

• My definition of student leadership (before reading the book)...

• My definition of student leadership (after reading the book)...

• After reading the book, I learned...

• If I knew I could do anything for God and not fail, it would be...

Today's date:

Chapter One

Student Leaders Serve

Radical leadership

If you asked the president of a large company for a one-word definition of leadership, she might describe it as *enthusiasm, drive, power, presence,* or *competence.* These words are often associated with the world's view of leadership.

But if you investigate Jesus' leadership requirements for his closest followers, you'll see that only one word makes it to the top of his list. It's not an attractive word that will make you want to race to the end of this book. Ready? Drum roll, please...Jesus asked his leaders to... *serve.* Serve! (Go ahead and reread it—I'll wait.)

Is it safe to assume that right now you're not too sure you want to be a leader if that's what leaders do? I understand—it's quite shocking at first. But if you want to follow the lead of Jesus, you'll find the primary objective of a biblical leader is to serve. Carefully read this verse to understand how Jesus wants his closest followers to act:

You know that in this world kings are tyrants, and officials lord it over the people beneath them. But among you it should be quite different. Whoever wants to be a leader among you must be your servant... (Matthew 20:25-26, NLT)

Jesus' selection of leaders could be considered either insane or ingenious. But since he was God in the flesh, let's assume his leadership judgment fits in the latter category. The first 12 men he chose to lead with him included five fishermen, a tax collector, and six others whose occupations are a complete mystery. Sometimes we wonder why Jesus chose these men instead of those who were already seen as leaders. Whatever the reason, the greatest leader ever to live chose ordinary guys to lead with him.

Clearly, Jesus connected serving to leading. He deepened the definition of leadership when he described himself as a servant rather than a king:

"For even I, the Son of Man, came here not to be served but to serve others, and to give my life as a ransom for many" (Matthew 20:28, NLT).

Jesus didn't just speak about serving; he modeled it. He put the needs of others first and placed himself in positions where serving was necessary. Ultimately, this posture of servanthood led him to the cross—to serve the needs of humanity. He served without reservation, and the greatest act of servanthood was also the greatest act of leadership our world has ever seen.

Think about that for a moment. Jesus. God in the flesh. All-powerful, all-knowing, all God, and yet, all servant—to everyone! He served the down and out, the sinner, the outcast, the lonely, and the poor. Leader? Yes. Servant? Absolutely!

As Jesus served, he created and led a movement with the potential to influence others! Given Jesus' actions, my definition of leadership would include two key words: *serve* and *influence*. Jesus did both. That's leadership!

If you want to be a leader—not just a student leader, but a Christian leader—you must learn to lead like Jesus. How? By serving others. When you serve others, you'll have the opportunity not only to lead, but also to change the image of leadership in your church, in your youth group, in your family, and in your school.

So instead of viewing your leadership role as a chance to exert power and voice your opinions, view it as an opportunity to serve. When you do, you'll succeed at leadership, and you'll grow to be more like Jesus.

Serve...like Jesus

The apostle Paul emphasized Jesus' servanthood and humility when he challenged Christians with the following words:

> Your attitude should be the same as that of Christ Jesus: Who, being in very nature God, did not consider equality with God something to be grasped, but made himself nothing, taking the very nature of a servant, being made in human likeness. (Philippians 2:5-7)

Paul told early Christians to be like Jesus (except for the perfection part—which is too bad since walking on water and casting out demons could be scary and fun). What does it mean to be like Jesus? It's more than wearing a WWJD (What Would Jesus Do) logo…it means taking on his character—being a servant.

As you read this book carefully, you'll see that leadership and service go hand in hand. (I desperately want you to understand this concept before you move on to the next chapter.) As a student leader, if you want to be effective, you'll need to serve others.

Many church-based student leadership programs are populated by the cute, fun, and outgoing kids who win popularity contests within the youth group. That's the wrong way to choose student leaders. Leadership is not about popularity; it's about…guess what? Serving. If you don't serve others, you're not a Christian leader. I don't care how popular, charismatic, and wonderful you are…if you want to be a leader, you must be a servant. Get it? (Got it!) Good!

Several students were immediately interested when I began to float the idea of creating a student leadership group at our church. But at our first informational meeting, I emphasized that biblical leadership (and leading like Jesus) requires servanthood and humility. Being a biblical leader wouldn't necessarily mean one would have popularity and power. My words disappointed many students. After that meeting there was a lot less excitement about leadership. Several students wanted to be leaders because they thought they'd be in front of the crowd, make important choices that would affect the ministry calendar, and be consulted on youth group decisions. Servanthood never occurred to them.

Our student leadership team was small at the start because very few students were willing to serve. Few were willing to pick up trash, stack chairs, and go out of their way to befriend disinterested and lonely students. In other words, I had a lot of students who wanted to be known as leaders…but not many who wanted to serve as leaders. We were learning about the big difference between biblical and worldly leadership.

The backbone of Christian leadership is simple to understand yet very difficult to pull off: Serve. Master this task, and you'll become a powerful student leader. (If *servant* doesn't describe you right now, don't give up. Just keep reading and pray for God to mold you into the type of leader he wants you to become. Stay with me through the end of the book. I will challenge you, but I'll be nice, too. I promise.)

Even me?

I posed the following question to a small group of students: "Who do you recognize as God's leaders?" Most of the group thought I was asking a tricky question. A ninth grader named Jackson responded, "God's leaders are, like, those spiritual giants who have it all together and haven't sinned in, like, five years." Thankfully, Jackson was wrong.

I was excited to teach Jackson and his peers that all of God's leaders are imperfect and unqualified. Do you think that's good news? Do those words describe you—imperfect? Unqualified? (Yeah, me too!)

The Bible doesn't present one clear description of what a leader looks like. What God reveals to us about leaders through the Scriptures is full of variety and imperfection. Here's a quick glance at a few people God used to do great things:

• **Jonah:** God told him to preach in Nineveh, and he disobeyed. He went in the opposite direction, and yet God used Jonah to move an entire city away from evil.

• **Abraham:** He lied to protect himself (which almost cost him his wife). But he believed God's promise, and God called him righteous because of his faith. Abraham is considered the father of the Jewish nation.

• **David:** He committed adultery, fathered a child out of wedlock, had an innocent man killed to cover his sin, and sought God's forgiveness. But still God called him "a man after my own heart" (Acts 13:22). For hundreds of years kings were evaluated according to the standard set by David.

• **Peter:** He was an impulsive disciple of Jesus who, in order to save himself, denied he knew Jesus. Peter's mouth got him into trouble. Yet God used him to build the early church.

God used disobedient liars, adulterers, big mouths, and fearful people. Isn't that amazing? Now, knowing that, do you think he can use you? Of course he can! God specializes in turning losers into leaders (just ask my parents, friends, and children).

Don't be so consumed with your past that you lose sight of what God can do with you now and in the future. When you understand that God can transform a murderer into a minister (Acts 9:1-31) and a prostitute into a protector of God's chosen people (Joshua 2:1-23), you'll know God can use you, too—blemishes and all.

After I shared this truth with my group, Jackson said, "Doug, when you give examples like that, it makes me think God doesn't care about my behavior. It seems like I can go out and do wild stuff, and God will still use me to be a leader." While Jackson made a fair statement, it's not an accurate one. Of course God cares about your actions. But if God used only perfect people, then Jesus would be the only biblical leader ever to have lived.

God has standards, and the Bible characters described previously were transformed when they humbled themselves before their God. They had to deal with the consequences of their actions, but God still used their imperfections and their humility to do great things.

The most likely candidate for leadership is the person who submits his life to God humbly, puts the needs of others before his own needs, and has a genuine desire to serve. Are you willing to do that? When you give up your own desire to be built up in exchange for serving God, you'll be amazed at the results. You will be blessed, Jesus will be glorified, and others will grow closer to God.

Because God uses flawed people, today's leaders possess a variety of broken backgrounds. God finds ways to use them when their hearts are right, and when they're willing to serve.

Congratulations! You have what it takes to be a leader for God.

Do it quietly

Each week Taylor arrives early to set up chairs and tables for our weekly service. After he's done with that job, he puts pens and fliers on each table. Taylor's devoted himself to this job for about two years now. I think I'm the only one who knows he does this. Taylor is the kind of guy who doesn't want others to see his acts of service. He's not doing these jobs for the praise of his friends; he's committed to serving God.

Taylor's reward for his service is evident when I see the expression on his face as students begin to arrive. As they use the chairs and tables, read the fliers, and write with the pens, Taylor feels a sense of pride—not an arrogant pride, but a servant's sense of accomplishment as he gets to see his impact felt. He feels ownership for our ministry because he's made an investment with his time, heart, and service.

What I appreciate so much about Taylor are the ways his acts of service influence others. Yet Taylor doesn't serve to get credit. That's a picture of true servanthood: Don't serve for the recognition; serve out of obedience to God and allow that service to influence others. Plus, the praise you receive from humans can't compare to how God will bless your secret acts of service. Taylor embodies this principle of leadership because he understands the teachings of Jesus found in the following verses:

> Take care! Don't do your good deeds publicly, to be admired, because then you will lose the reward from your Father in heaven. When you give a gift to someone in need, don't shout about it as the hypocrites do—blowing trumpets in the synagogues and streets to call attention to their acts of charity! I assure you, they have received all the reward they will ever get. But when you give to someone, don't tell your left hand what your right hand is doing. Give your gifts in secret, and your Father, who knows all secrets, will reward you. (Matthew 6:1-4, NLT)

When you show up at your youth ministry, you make a choice to be a consumer (where you are served by others) or a minister (where you serve others). God will use you in great ways when you come to serve others. When you serve without seeking recognition, honor, or praise, you'll be rewarded in a way that rivals the praise other people can give you. Would you rather have one person say, "Good job!

Thanks!" or would you rather have God know your heart, see your service, and bless your life? The answer seems so obvious. When you do something for the praise of others, the praise will be short-lived and incomplete. When you serve out of obedience to God, you'll be rewarded in a way that's almost impossible to describe with words. Jesus put it this way: "...and your Father, who sees what is done in secret, will reward you" (Matthew 6:18).

God rewards your acts of service...your quiet obedience...your leadership through influence. God's reward system can't be defined, controlled, or manipulated. When you serve, you lead. And when you do, you'll tap into God's rich flow of blessings on your life.

A last leadership thought and challenge

I'm thrilled someone believed in you enough to put this book into your hands. I'm so proud of you for making the effort to learn about being a leader for God! I want you to be a leader, but more importantly, I want you to seek to honor God with your life. When you do, he'll bless your obedience, he'll reward your service, and he'll use you to influence others in ways you can't even begin to imagine.

Remember—leadership isn't about position, power, or prestige...it's about serving God and others. You can do that—I know you can! The challenge is to keep reading and learning—and looking for ways you can lead through your service. You can be a leader!

Alyssa's Notes

Honestly, when I first read this chapter, I thought, "Okay, great. I know being a leader means serving. I've heard it before; I'll hear it again. Just get on with another point." Then God convicted me of my pride a few minutes later. I realized that so much of the time I think of myself as a student leader who serves instead of defining my leadership as serving all the time. As Doug kept describing Jesus as our model leader and servant, I felt challenged to start striving to make serving a lifestyle, not something I do every once in a while. It's hard to serve all the time, but by striving to do this, we are inviting God to use us in amazing ways.

Chapter Two

Student Leaders Serve...in Big Ways

After reading Chapter One, you shouldn't be surprised to find a challenge to serve others when you dig into this chapter. You'll be excited to learn that serving in big ways doesn't really take that much effort. Big serving opportunities aren't really that big—it's the little things that become big acts of service! Are you confused? You won't be as you read about some powerful ways you can enhance your leadership...and they're really not that difficult.

Serve 'til it's over

When you help plan an event and are excited to see it happen, the planning doesn't feel like work. Sure there's effort involved, but since you're anxious for the event to happen, your labor and anticipation mix together to form an enjoyable experience. But when the event ends, and it's time to clean up the mess, it's natural to lose your enthusiasm. Many people who helped set up the event will try to slip out of the cleanup phase (early exit...stage left).

Student leaders need to understand that both the setup and cleanup of an event are very important parts of a ministry program. Every one of your youth ministry programs consists of before, during, and after. The *during* is interesting and exciting, the *before* is fun because of the anticipation, but the *after* can be boring work.

I ask our student leaders to commit to arriving early to help set up. And I ask them not to leave until the entire event is finished—which means after the mess is cleaned up. When we stick together, we rejoice as leaders in our common tasks and commitment. That's so much better than the typical scenario of one person doing all the work and leaving the event feeling lonely, too tired to rejoice, and having just enough energy to feel bitterness toward the others who didn't stay around to help. It may not sound like much, but believe me…staying 'til it's really over is a big act of service.

When you take the initiative in this area, you'll breathe life into other leaders—especially the leader in charge. Continually coaxing students into fulfilling the *after* responsibilities becomes tiring and frustrating. When the burden of the entire program is shared, you'll create a positive teamwork environment. Plus, when everyone works together, the job gets done quickly. Surprisingly enough, when a boring job is done with a positive attitude, even the *after* can become a lot of fun. And when a job is fun, others will want to be involved, too.

I'll never forget the time Alison, a student leader, told me to leave an event before everything was cleaned up. She wanted me to spend some time with my children before they went to bed. Alison promised to make sure everything was put away. She actually sent her youth pastor home by literally forcing me out the door. I was amazed and honored by her actions (and, to be honest, a little scared I would return the next day and be in trouble because they had left a big mess). Fortunately, Alison and our other leaders not only did a great job of cleaning up, but also they gave me the gift of additional time with my children. I was encouraged, my family was happier, and Alison gained a new level of my respect and the respect of our other leaders. Alison's small gesture of service made a big difference. Try it yourself sometime. Stick around until an event is completely over, have fun by sending your youth pastor home, and maybe you'll be mentioned in a book. (Alison, you're the best!)

Hey, no one is doing that

I recognize a student leader when I see someone serving in the tasks most people run from. I look at the person and think, "She's either a student leader, or she's being punished for something." A leader serves even when no one else will help.

Imagine this scene: Students are clearing tables and washing dishes after a youth ministry event. Over in a corner of the room, a little out of sight, sits a trashcan. Ignoring this trashcan is very easy to do. It's overloaded with cups and plates and leaking a nasty, greenish-yellow punch goop. You see it and immediately categorize it under the heading of "disgusting, gross, foul, demonic-like, and putrid." You think, "Yikes, someone is really going to be bummed while cleaning up that mess!"

What would a servant leader do in this situation? Well, because emptying this disgusting trashcan is a job that must be done, she'd break away from the group project and clean up the mess without being asked and without seeking recognition. She'd solve the problem and do the unthinkable. (No, not drink it. And, although it might be funny, she wouldn't hide the trashcan in the senior pastor's office.) A servant leader tackles the problem head on and cleans it up.

When it's party time and your gang of friends is involved, it's much easier to serve. But you'll become a stronger student leader every time you do something no one else is willing to do. I value the student leader who serves in unflattering ways without being asked and without begging others to help. When I see one of our leaders act this way, I thank God for her leadership. I feel a sense of spiritual pride that there's a teenager in our ministry who *gets it*. She understands that a leader serves…I love it!

When you give extra attention to the tasks that would otherwise go unnoticed, you're an encouragement to all the leaders because you're sharing the ministry load. Serving in this way is a sign of your spiritual maturity, and it's a display of your dedication to lead through serving.

As you take initiative to help in these situations, you'll see it's these small tasks that help build big character traits in your life. When you take responsibility for the tasks others run from, you communicate your willingness to do what it takes to be used by God. So what if it's a nasty trash can? Go for it. What's the worst that can happen? When I see students' dependability in the little things, I know they'll be faithful in the bigger tasks as they come along. Those are the people I'll use. I rely on student leaders who've shown initiative and faithfulness in the small projects no one else wanted to do. Becoming aware of needs and meeting them, even when you have to do it alone, is a big step of service and an important step in your leadership development.

Be a clique buster, part one

The best youth group in the world appears cliquey to the student who doesn't know anyone, doesn't fit in, or feels uncomfortable. Occasionally cliques are positive things—especially if you're part of one. But usually most cliques have a negative influence because others feel excluded. Cliques happen when genuine fellowship turns ugly. When it's ugly, everyone hates it…but few people do anything about cliques. This is a place where, as a student leader, I want you to be different.

I pray you'll be the type of leader who not only cares about this problem, but also who does something to break down the cliques in your youth group. God will use your leadership in a great way when you become a clique buster. If you look outside your group of friends to find those who aren't connected, people will be helped, you'll grow in your leadership skills, and God will be honored.

Please don't misunderstand what I'm saying. I want you to have friends who you have fun with, who build you up, and who really care about the condition of your faith. Those relationships are key to a healthy, long-term faith! But sometimes that group of Christian friends needs to say, "Ready, break!" and rush from their friendship huddle to look for those who are alone or isolated. They need to hang out with these people and find ways to get them connected to others in the larger group.

Often when the subjects of greeting others and breaking up cliques come up in a leadership meeting, student leaders will shout in support of these ideas: "Yeah, we really shouldn't be so cliquey!" But many times the student leaders are the source of the clique problem. These leaders are well connected, liked, and too busy hanging out with their friends to notice those who aren't well connected.

I challenge you to evaluate your own cliquey-ness before you talk about it with other student leaders. Is there anything you're able to change about yourself before you begin identifying the faults of others within the youth ministry? You'll be amazed by how other student leaders follow your lead when you say, "Hey, let's go meet some new people and talk with those who have no one to talk to." As each student leader begins to reach out to others, cliques will disappear quickly. But stay on your guard... they can return very easily, too.

Be a clique buster, part two

If we sat down face-to-face, we'd probably agree that cliques are dangerous to youth groups. And we'd agree student leaders have great potential to successfully break them up. But agreeing about a problem (and its solution) and actually solving it require different commitments.

Let's identify three commitments that will strengthen your existing friendships, help break down cliques, and add to the health of your youth ministry. Be the type of leader who doesn't just talk about the problem—do something about it! Let me give you some ideas on how to be that kind of leader.

Commitment #1: *Commit to a regular meeting time when student leaders hang out together.* Have fun and hold each other accountable for personal spiritual growth. You don't have to meet weekly, but you should meet often enough to deepen the leadership relationships. (I suggest once a month.) This meeting shouldn't be an exclusive *holy huddle* time, but it should be a place where student leaders interact with other leaders, have fun with their friends, and receive some leadership training. Your clique-busting time will be easier if you know there will be other times when you'll be with your leader friends.

Commitment #2: *Commit to separating from each other.* At special events, Bible studies, and weekly youth programs, make a commitment to have no more than two student leaders together at the same time. Each pair works together to meet new people or talk with those who aren't leaders. By separating from the leadership group, you'll reach more people and erase the appearance of a leadership clique.

I know many students who've left church events because they walked into an unfriendly feeling room. And I know a lot of students who opened their hearts to Jesus because they felt comfortable and accepted when they entered the room. They were curious about what was behind all the warmth and friendliness. Do you know what it was? The power of God working through committed leaders who were more interested in serving others than in being comfortable and serving themselves.

Commitment #3: *Commit to being prepared to answer questions about the youth ministry program.* A great way to connect the unconnected to a youth ministry is to invite them to activities. To do this effectively, you need to know what's happening in your youth ministry and other important details (upcoming events, costs, dates, registration information, where to get information, if anyone cute is going—just kidding—etc.). When you're able to answer questions accurately, you increase your value as a leader and show others you really care about helping them get involved. You don't need to know every answer. If you don't know the answer to the question, say, "That's a great question. I don't know. Let's go find out together what the answer is." When you do this, you're making a personal connection and communicating concern for the other person.

Working to break up cliques will benefit you as much as it will benefit other students desperately wanting to belong and fit in. When these commitments become a natural part of your leadership routine, you'll find yourself influencing other students in ways you've never imagined. Your peers will be open to learning more about God when they feel welcomed and accepted in the group.

Be on the lookout

Let's pretend your youth ministry is clique free. Still there will be new students and even regularly attending students who'll feel alone at different times. As a leader you need to watch for these people. When you spot them, go meet them, talk to them, sit with them, and introduce them to others. That's what Jesus would do, and it's an action God will honor and reward.

Typically those on the outside feel uneasy because they want to be part of the action but are too uncomfortable to take the first scary step to do what it takes to connect with others. If you haven't experienced this feeling, please put yourself in an uncomfortable situation so you can identify with people who feel this way. Go visit another youth group where you don't know anyone. Then you'll know what really being alone feels like. When you feel this discomfort, you'll be more sensitive to helping people who have trouble fitting in. Feeling disconnected in a social situation feels uncomfortable and creates negative feelings about the group.

But everyone will feel good when you approach an disconnected person and talk to him. Watch his facial expression. His eyes will light up with anticipation. His words may be soft and brief, but he'll be thankful you cared enough to notice him. No one wants to stand in a room full of people and feel alone. Your attempt to make a personal connection is like throwing out a relationship life raft.

Once you've made the initial contact, don't look for a quick escape. I've watched student leaders with good intentions strike up a conversation with a loner and, at the first sign of an awkward pause, excuse themselves and go back to their friends. What's better is to say, "Come on. Let's meet some other people from the group." If you're turned down, don't be discouraged; it's probably because of their extreme discomfort and not because of your breath.

You don't need to feel like a baby sitter. If the person strikes up a conversation with someone you introduce him to, it's okay to excuse yourself and go meet someone else. As you do this repeatedly, it will become a more natural response. Making others feel comfortable is not an easy thing to do because most of the time we focus on our own comfort and not on the discomfort of others. But it's a small act of service that gets big results...every time.

Diffuse...don't fuel

As a leader in a youth ministry, you'll find yourself in the middle of chaotic situations at times. Churches are filled with people, and where there are people, there will be problems, confusion, hurt, chaos, and youth pastors with corny jokes. Frustration is a natural response to chaos. The next time this happens to you, diffuse the situation by deciding to help in a positive way instead of adding fuel to the problems with thoughtless actions.

A few years ago I planned a summer camp on houseboats on a lake in Arizona. I'd organized this trip several times in the past, but this one particular summer the trip turned into a nightmare. A rainstorm forced us off our houseboats. Chaos arrived! (And we didn't see it coming.) A borrowed ski boat sank during the storm, there was no dry place for us to seek refuge, and our students were screaming, scared, and confused. We were in trouble with very few options—the situation seemed hopeless.

So...how would you choose to diffuse (or fuel) this chaos? You diffuse the problem by being helpful in any way you can. I remember 16-year-old Michael asking me, "Doug, what can I do to help?" I appreciated this leader's desire, but there was nothing he could do at that moment. I asked him to be mellow and stay calm. I explained that his calmness would help settle others down. He sat with some of his buddies, and his relaxed posture and attitude helped diffuse some of the tension.

Another student, Jillian, chose to enliven the event because people were being "too serious" (her words). She started a water fight among those trying to salvage the sunken ski boat. Jillian's actions fueled the crisis (and she became a target for several leaders who desired to bury her inside the sunken boat). Two different leaders, two different options, two different outcomes. The valued leader is the one who diffuses the situation. Choose to diffuse chaotic situations when you have the opportunity. And you will—probably sooner than you might imagine: Chaos is around every corner.

Every youth ministry has at least one person who will react inappropriately to difficult situations. As a leader you must have a positive attitude when ministry becomes difficult...which it will. All church ministries experience tough times. For example, when the van driver gets lost and his frustration is obvious, this is not the time to make funny comments highlighting his driving mistakes. Student leaders refrain from doing this. Although the teasing may appear to be a harmless laugh, it fuels the tension the driver already feels.

When other leaders know you can be counted on to help work out problems, you'll gain credibility and earn the right to be trusted during future chaotic times. When I've been in the middle of difficult situations, I find joy in having other leaders who take direction well, help make important decisions, and make a positive contribution until the storm passes. When your ministry encounters chaos, be ready to serve by diffusing the tension. I guarantee your sensitivity to the difficulty of the situation will make a huge difference in its outcome.

The mother of all ministry

A wise person once said, "Necessity is the mother of invention." This means anyone can become an inventor when something is really needed. The guy who invented the eraser saw a huge need for correcting his mistakes. He responded to the need by inventing something used a million times every day (thousands of times each day by me).

A student leader becomes very helpful when she looks for needs and finds ways to meet them. Needs—the mother of all ministry. Can you think of any needs in your youth ministry? You discover needs by keeping your eyes and ears open to what's happening around you and what people are saying. Always ask important questions about what you see and hear.

While I was writing this book, I met with Alex, one of our student leaders. I asked him to look for needs in our ministry for one week, come back to see me at the church, and ask me three questions based on his active discovery of our ministry needs. Here are the three great questions he asked:

• **When the adults have a volunteer meeting, who watches their children?**

• **If students have been absent for a week or two, who calls to check on them?**

• **If people are gossiping, who speaks up to say it's wrong?**

Great questions! Each question reveals a critical need within our youth ministry. Now, we've devised a pretty good plan for dealing with Alex's second question (he just didn't know what it was). But the other two questions point to real areas of weakness in parts of our ministry. As we discussed these two needs, I asked Alex for his ideas about how we might meet them. If we meet these needs, we'll save our adult leaders money spent on childcare and help them feel valued, and we'll stop damaging rumors from spreading. These are important issues to deal with, and I'm so thankful Alex identified them.

Now don't misinterpret this idea. Don't start walking around your youth group with a clipboard, pointing out problems and writing them down. But be alert for and aware of needs as you encounter them. If you try this for a couple of weeks and can't identify any needs, ask your main leader for help. Just say, "I want to be more sensitive to identifying needs in our youth group. Right now I can't see any. Will you give me an example of one?" Using examples helps train your eyes, ears, and heart to notice some needs you are walking past every week.

Alex came back to see me the following week with another question. A few weeks later he asked another question. Alex got it. He understood that our youth ministry isn't about him...or you...or me: It's about us. All leaders need to keep their eyes open and look for ways to serve others by meeting these needs.

You don't have to be a superhero to make a huge impact in ministry. Often all it takes is becoming aware of needs and finding ways to meet them through serving.

A last leadership thought and challenge

I want you to understand that big leadership happens through relatively small actions. I'm not asking you to go build new church buildings; I'm asking you to notice someone who isn't connected, break down cliques, and do things others aren't doing. I challenge you to go back through this chapter and skim the section headings, go over the main points again, and then grade yourself on your current status related to each of these small ideas.

Identify one of these actions and put it on your mental radar screen starting right now. Don't wait 'til the end of the book. Make it a priority right now to improve in that one area. You can always go back to the other sections and work on those later. Just pick one small area where you can begin to see big results. Use the list below to help with the evaluation process. Don't be too hard on yourself as you evaluate your current leadership status. If we were hanging out together, I'd tell you to give yourself a higher grade. (But then again, if we were hanging out, that would be weird because I'm old).

F: Ouch...this doesn't describe me at all.
D: Well...I've done that before, but it's not a regular action.
C: Okay...I think about it more than I do it.
B: Good...I'm more on the good side than the okay side.
A: Great...this does describe who I am and what I do.

_____ **Serve 'til it's over.**
_____ **Hey, no one is doing that!**
_____ **Be a clique buster.**
_____ **Be on the lookout.**
_____ **Diffuse...don't fuel.**
_____ **The mother of all ministry (identify/meet needs)**

Star the action you're going to focus on immediately.

Alyssa's Notes

One aspect of serving I have thought a lot about is cleaning up after church events. Just go pick up trash...right? I always get so frustrated and feel as if it isn't that easy. I feel like if I start cleaning up right away, everyone watches me and thinks I'm trying to draw attention to myself. Other student leaders have actually acted this way and even said negative things to me for cleaning up. But I'm learning two things through this frustration: First, encourage other student leaders. If for some reason I can't stay the extra 10 minutes that night, then I try to cheer on whoever can. Second, continue to clean up. I can't control what other people are thinking or saying. I can only keep my motives in check and keep serving.

Chapter Three

Student Leaders Deepen Their Faith

If you read only the first two chapters, you might be tempted to put this book down and think, "Okay, I get it. Leadership is about serving. I don't need to waste my time reading anymore. I need to get out there and serve." Well, that's too simplistic a response, and following through on it could be a big mistake.

While serving is essential to being a biblical leader, leadership requires more than serving—it also requires a right heart. Serving God through serving others is often referred to as *the work of the ministry*, and it reveals the part of a Christian's life seen by others. In this chapter we'll consider the part of your life that can't be seen by others. I'll challenge you to evaluate the condition of your inner world. A discussion of your inner world doesn't have to be mystical or spooky or weird. It's simply a term that helps describe your spiritual life—your heart, your faith, and your relationship with God. A healthy inner world (spiritual life) is vital to the Christian leader who wants to be used by God. A significant distinction between a student leader at a public school and a Christian student leader is the emphasis on a healthy faith connection with God.

If you try to serve God with a dry, empty, and weak heart, you'll lack the essential ingredient for effective, God-honoring leadership. Student leaders don't need to be perfect, but they do need to deepen their relationships with God and pay attention to their inner worlds so their outer worlds of service are genuine and reflect God's love.

This is a very important chapter for you. I pray this chapter will challenge you to consider your heart's condition. Think about being God's person even when you don't feel like it. Before you read any further, stop and ask God to use my broken and inadequate words to serve as a guide to a greater work and spiritual awakening in your life.

What happened to that feeling?

What is your goal for personal spiritual growth? If you went away on a long vacation (let's say three months), would you have what it takes to continue growing spiritually without your church's help? Would you identify yourself as someone capable of growing spiritually without your youth group programs?

I know a lot of teenagers who grow spiritually when they experience the spiritual high from summer camp or the warm feeling they get inside from singing a lot of songs about God. I know students who grow spiritually when they experience the comfort of being around adult leaders who ask them questions about their faith. These are great experiences; they help build spiritual foundations. But student leaders must learn to grow spiritually on their own. Those three words—*on your own*—are key to being a student leader who is connected to God and his power.

Personally, as a leader in ministry, I must be growing on my own. No one cares about my spiritual health as much as I do. So I've had to learn about and develop some spiritual disciplines that keep me connected to God, refresh my heart, and daily renew my commitment to follow God's ways. If I don't do this regularly, the result might be a weak and confused faith. I feel and see this through my thoughts and actions. If I'm going to be a leader, I must focus on my spiritual life.

Unfortunately, I've watched many student leaders graduate from their faith after they graduate from high school because they've left the comfort and closeness of a youth group. Their enthusiasm for serving God and working at the church diminishes, and soon their passion for following God does as well. It's sad but true. I'm sure you can name some friends you've watched this happen to.

As a leader, if you're not careful to monitor and watch the condition of your spiritual life, you'll become a Christian phony. Laura was a girl in my youth group who worked hard to maintain her Christian appearance. She had a cross tattoo on her arm. She wore her "I ♥ God" T-shirt, and she said the right words that seemed to indicate a spiritual maturity. But on the inside her heart was decaying, and her faith was immature. She focused on her external Christian look rather than tending to her internal depth. Her spiritual life became shallow and hollow. Jesus has strong words for this type of phony faith. Read these words carefully:

> Then the Lord [Jesus] said to him, "You Pharisees are so careful to clean the outside of the cup and the dish, but inside you are still filthy—full of greed and wickedness! Fools! Didn't God make the inside as well as the outside?" (Luke 11:39-40, NLT)

Jesus was concerned his followers would only pay attention to their actions (serving others) and neglect their inner worlds. The inner world—your spiritual life—is the source of your actions. Jesus says the mere words that come from our mouths originate and come from our hearts: "A good person produces good words from a good heart, and an evil person produces evil words from an evil heart" (Matthew 12:35, NLT).

Please pay special attention to the condition of your spiritual life. But don't confuse passion with feeling. There will be times in your relationship with God when you may not feel close to him. That's normal—you're not alone in that feeling. But you can still be passionate about God and growing in your relationship with him even when the feeling isn't there. Following God, loving him, and serving passionately are acts of obedience not based on feeling.

Here's an example: Many times I don't feel like doing the right thing. I may not feel like loving my neighbor today, but because I'm passionate about obeying and following Jesus, I choose to obey God's command and love my neighbor—even when I don't feel like it.

To help deepen your passion for God, I encourage you to find another student leader to meet with regularly. Use this time to discuss your faith's passion. Personally, I take great strides in my spiritual journey when I connect with others who are passionate about following Jesus. When you're around others who exude passion, you'll find it contagious, and you'll want it to rub off on your life.

Now that's attractive

"Pride goes before destruction..." (Proverbs 16:18, NLT) A great example of the meaning of this verse is found when one watches the prebout hype of any high-profile boxing match. These multimillionaire athletes boast about their talent, strength, and sheer dominance over their opponents. Then fast-forward to the end of the bout, and you'll find one superstar bruised, bleeding, defeated, and no longer boasting. It's a visual display of pride coming before destruction.

I see nothing attractive about arrogance, and I see clearly the attractiveness of humility. When someone displays the quiet, controlled confidence of humility, it's a good look. I believe it's one of the most attractive qualities Christians can possess. I want student leaders to pursue humility. Why? Humility is a sign of a spiritually mature heart. Humility reveals a heart that has been cared for by the growing leader.

Humility is found in someone who knows God and experiences his unconditional and undeserved love. Humility flows from a confidence in God's love and acceptance. The humble leader doesn't need to brag, show off, or convince anyone of his greatness. He's able to display humility because he's confident God is in charge, and he's not.

The attractive quality of humility is not developed overnight. It's a unique quality in that you can't tell people you've arrived at humility. The minute you tell someone you're humble...you're not humble! True humility is observed, not trumpeted for everyone to hear. Humility is expressed in the life of one who is growing in her inner world.

So the next time you want to boast but choose not to...you've made a move toward humility. Every time you serve someone, you make another move toward humility. Keep making those moves, and God will transform your heart from one that wants to be known to a heart that wants God to be known...that's humility. Look for it in others...it's very attractive. "Pride ends in humiliation, while humility brings honor" (Proverbs 29:23, NLT).

The foundation for right choices

I've noticed that students who pay attention to their inner lives have something in common with each other—they tend to live lives committed to obeying God's word.

It's difficult to live God's way. I'm thankful the Bible includes illustrations of spiritual knuckleheads who disobeyed God and brought a lot of pain into their lives. Luckily, these same knuckleheads had their lives transformed by God and became shining examples to follow. I'm glad God put people in the Bible who made mistakes and yet used those same people in amazing ways when they surrendered their lives completely to his ways.

When you were given this book, you may have felt a little unworthy to consider being a leader used by God. Actually, I hope you do feel a little unworthy...because that's the quality of humility that makes a leader attractive. Humility, combined with a sincere passion to serve God, is a powerful combination God uses—especially when that leader makes decisions based on Scripture.

There's a great relationship between right choices and an honored life: Godly choices result in a godly life, and a godly life creates more godly choices! And the Bible makes it very clear that God honors right choices.

Right choices are easier to make when you're filling your heart with God's Word. This shouldn't be difficult to understand. If the Bible is my guide, then I can test my choices through the grid of my guide. One of God's intentions for the Scriptures is to help make our choices easier. Look at these classic verses from the Old Testament:

Do not let this Book of the Law depart from your mouth; meditate on it day and night, so that you may be careful to do everything written in it. Then you will be prosperous and successful. (Joshua 1:8, NIV)

> How can a young person stay pure? By obeying
> your word and following its rules. (Psalm 119:9,
> NLT)

It's obvious that God's Word is given to you and me so
we might know right from wrong and as a guide to help
us live life to its fullest. God created you to be effective,
secure, and content when you follow his ways. When you
commit to living a life reflecting godly choices, you'll be
more satisfied with your life, and you'll feel your life is
ready for God to use as he pleases.

Yeah, I'm serious

Are you catching the essence of this chapter? I sure hope
so! As a ministry leader, you must continue to grow in
your relationship with God and in knowledge of his
ways. A growing faith is crucial for a growing leader. But
spiritual growth won't happen automatically. Growth
requires time with God. Time with God happens alone,
with others, at church, during service opportunities, and
through ministry. You spend time with God when you
read and consume God's Word.

I'm so thankful God left us with his instruction
manual on living life to its fullest. Typically, most teenagers
don't get excited about the challenge to read.

"Hey, Cody, let's read!"

"Oh, thanks, Doug, I'm thrilled for the offer
to read. I'm glad you're saving me from the horrors of

eating ice cream, going to the movies, and hanging out with my friends!"

Okay, I understand reading can be a chore. But while some of your spiritual growth will come as a result of relationships, life experience, and ministry, there's something rewarding about reading God's Word and his living instructions. I challenge you to become a student of God's Word.

If you don't read the Bible now, try reading one minute a day and build on that time each day.[1] Begin with small steps to develop an appetite for God's Word that will turn your Bible reading into a lifelong habit.

As you read the Bible, you'll gain knowledge (information) and acquire wisdom (knowing how to react to information) that will help you become a stronger leader. The book of Proverbs tells us that knowledge and wisdom are more valuable than silver or gold (3:13-14 and 16:16). Interesting, huh? Just imagine the riches you'll gain from reading the Bible!

Fuel for your inner world

Because I've seen it happen too many times, I can't remember the number of student leaders who spent years in our youth ministry and then graduated from their faith. There are few things that discourage me as much as this trend. Do you know anyone who fits that description? I sure don't want this to happen to you.

---

[1] (I wrote a one-year devotional that goes with a one-year Bible reading plan. It's called *One-Minute Bible 4 Students*, and it's a great tool to help you develop an appetite for God's Word—check it out at www.simplyyouthministry.com.)

Why does a spiritual life fall apart when the safety of the youth group is gone? I'm sure there are several answers to that question, but the most apparent answer is that most of the students who graduate from their faith didn't learn how to grow on their own during their teenage years. That's where I want you to be different!

Many students experienced spiritual growth when they had a youth program to attend or a person to hold them accountable for their spiritual lives. But because they hadn't built their own solid spiritual foundations, their faith crumbled when the programs and the people were gone.

In an attempt to attack this problem, I sat down with older Christian men and women who have been faithfully following God's ways for 40 or more years. I asked them, "How have you been able to maintain a deep faith throughout the years?" Then, based on their responses, I began to focus on some of the spiritual habits these mature Christians identified for me. They had some answers in common: Spend time with God, connect with other believers, study and memorize God's Word, and give time and tithes to the church. These habits served as the foundations of their faith.

Because I didn't want my students (especially my student leaders) to graduate from their faith when they left the youth group, I attempted to pass on to them what I learned from these godly men and women. I identified six common spiritual habits and described them in language easy to remember. (At least, I thought it was!)

H — Hang out with God
A — Accountable with another believer
B — Bible memorization
I — Involved with the church body
T — Tithe
S — Study Scripture

I don't care if you choose these six habits, find 42 new ones, or focus on one…what I challenge you to do is to make sure you develop some faith habits that will help you grow spiritually on your own. I love the words the apostle Paul wrote to the followers of Christ he loved so much: "Therefore, my dear friends, as you have always obeyed—not only in my presence, but now much more in my absence…" (Philippians 2:12, NIV). *In my absence.* What great words for you to hear as you strengthen your spiritual life as a young leader. Focus your heart for leading today and prepare your heart for spiritual growth *on your own* and *in the absence* of your current youth ministry leadership team tomorrow. If you don't graduate from your faith, you'll set a great example for others who follow you, and you'll be a leader who leads from an active faith.

Be ready to start your own church

How did you react when you read the heading for this section? Do you really think I want everyone who reads this book to start a church? Not necessarily. But I do want student leaders to be so strong in their faith that when they graduate high school and move on to college, they'll be spiritually strong enough to start a church if they can't find one to attend.

You might be thinking, "Seriously? Me? Start a church?" Yes. I want you to be so committed to your inner world (your spiritual life) and deepening your love for God that you'd do anything to keep him number one...even if it means starting a church.

When Jesus was gone from earth, the early followers gathered in homes to worship God—that was church. Church is simply a family of believers who gather together. Wherever Christians gather to worship God, church is taking place. If you can't find a church where you can worship, go gather some believers and start a church—a gathering of Christians.

But I want you to make a strong commitment to get involved with an existing church before you start your own...or be clear about God's call for you to start a church. Either way, make it a goal to be a strong enough Christian that you'd become a church planter if there were no churches in your area. Remember that the reason to start a church isn't to give you a platform for your leadership; it's to give God a platform for his leadership! A place to worship him, a place to serve others, a place to grow deeper, a place to strengthen relationships, and a place where non-Christians feel safe to find out more about God and his incredible love. In order to be capable of building something such as this, your faith needs to be developed and deepened right now.

One of my former students took this challenge seriously. Aaron didn't feel like there was a ministry in our area designed to reach his generation (students in their twenties who were curious about Christ). He was in his later twenties when he started Sakred—a church in South Orange County, California. I visited the church last Easter and was blown away by how God is using a former youth group kid to do something so important.

Aaron began preparing his heart when he was a high school student. God used his journey to prepare him to pastor others. As Aaron's youth pastor, I am overcome with joy that he took this challenge seriously. He is a better man because of the experience, and people are coming to know Jesus because of Aaron's spiritual growth and leadership determination.

One of your tasks as a student leader is to prepare yourself to serve God in great ways. Again, I don't know if that means starting a church...that's not the point. The point is how well you focus on your heart's condition. You need to get your heart in such good shape that if God were to call you to do something scary, big, and life changing (say, starting a church), you would be completely prepared for the spiritual journey ahead of you. Your heart's condition is the difference between being an effective student leader and being an ordinary student leader.

God wants to use you in ministry, but he's more concerned about a growing relationship with you than using you. Being used as a leader for God is the wonderful result of being personally connected with God and deepening your faith.

A last leadership thought and challenge

I've written this entire book pretending you are a student leader in my youth group. I haven't been writing to a nameless, distant teenager I'll never meet. Instead I've imagined you and me sitting across from one another at a fast-food place, drinking sodas, and talking about life, ministry, and leadership. This chapter is the point in our conversation where I sit on the edge of my seat, lean over the table, look you even deeper in the eyes and, with as much passion as I can communicate, say, "There's nothing more important for leaders to develop than their relationships with God. I'm thrilled to give you leadership ideas and encourage your gifts, but if you don't get this… you're missing the main thing. The main thing is to keep the main thing the main thing. It's all about God and your heart."

I want you to be a successful leader…but more than that I want you to know God. As you read this sentence, I challenge you to pray and tell God you desperately want to know him and grow into a deeper relationship with him. Then I'd like you to write God a letter describing the type of spiritual leader you want to become. Okay?

I'm proud of you for reading this far—you're a third of the way done. Way to go!

Alyssa's Notes

Growing in my relationship with God in spite of the busyness of life is one of my biggest struggles. It's so easy to get wrapped up in life and stop deepening my faith. I usually start doing one church event after another, and all of a sudden I become too busy to even know how I'm doing spiritually. Too often I don't even realize the areas I need to improve or grow in until they get out of control. So one important thing to me is setting aside time to really evaluate my relationship with God. I've found that when I make the effort to simply analyze and think about how I'm doing spiritually, it helps me immensely.

Chapter Four

Student Leaders Support
Their Ministries and Other Leaders

Let's do a quick review of the previous three chapters:

    • You got a picture of leadership that's not about power or popularity, but all about serving.

    • Then you saw that as you serve in small, even unnoticed ways, God takes your acts of service and produces big results.

    • Then I tried to get across the truth that the difference between an ordinary leader and a Christian leader is God's input. If you're going to grow as a Christian leader, you've got to tend to your spiritual life (inner world) and make fresher and deeper connections with God.

    Okay, are you ready for more? Of course you are—you're a growing leader anxious to learn and do more…right? While you're serving others and focusing on your spiritual life, I want to coach you to take time to understand more about your church, your youth ministry, and other leaders. When you understand what's happening in a particular ministry and why people do what they do, you'll benefit personally (you'll become more effective) and your church will benefit (you'll contribute as a team player).

Doing ministry with others is so much more fun than doing it alone. One huge highlight of my life has been working with other men and women with whom I've had the privilege of sharing ministry leadership. I want you to have that privilege, and I want other leaders to know you're on their side.

Support the *why* behind the *what*

Did you know that every event in your youth ministry serves a bigger purpose? The mud volleyball tournament, summer camp, and the Wednesday-night service would be pointless if they were simply ways to fill up your schedule and keep you busy.

As a student leader you'll need to move from being a mere program attendee to being a leader who is part of a bigger team. Let's say the youth ministry team at your church is responsible for the spiritual growth of teenagers... guess what? You have a part to play in that responsibility. Taking on that responsibility means you need to have an understanding of the purpose behind each program. Then you'll have fewer questions and complaints about your youth ministry and more enthusiasm and ideas to help make it better. Also, knowing the purpose of each program will help you be less of a spectator and more of a leader who can leverage your peer relationships to help fulfill each program's purpose.

Let's see how this might work. Pretend the primary purpose behind an upcoming church basketball tournament is to reach out to unchurched teenagers in your community and expose them to your youth group. When you understand this purpose, you'll be more likely to invite your friends who enjoy basketball but don't attend church. What happens if you don't know the purpose behind the program? Chances are you'll be tempted to complain that the church isn't emphasizing your favorite sport, and because of that, you won't participate in the event because basketball is a stupid sport compared to your favorite—synchronized swimming.

At our church the students who don't understand the purpose of a program are easy to identify because they're usually complaining. Almost always the complaining students are our regular attendees who don't like our Saturday night program. Many of our students are comfortable bringing their unchurched friends to our Saturday program (a highly relational time that's both fun and challenging). With a Bible lesson we include fun elements such as dramas, videos, and occasionally a game or crowd breaker. But the complaining students wish it were a spiritually deeper and more serious program. (By the way, these are the same students who never bring any of their unchurched friends.) Their complaints might have some validity if we never offered a program where they could experience more Bible study depth and be in a more serious environment. But in our church there is another program held on Wednesday nights designed specifically for those who want to go deeper with their faith. These complainers want depth on Saturday, too, when we have our largest crowd. Their complaint reveals a selfish I-want-what-I-want-when-I-want-it attitude. The bottom line is, they're not leaders. They're selfish consumers. If I heard our student leaders complaining like that, I would be very disappointed.

Public complaints about the purpose of a youth ministry program should never come from student leaders. If a leader wants to complain, he should schedule a meeting with the lead youth worker and share his concerns in a way that won't create division. Our student leaders fully recognize Saturday nights as times either to bring an unchurched friend or to show up with servant hearts and help do what it takes to welcome others and introduce them to the life-changing power and love of God.

Please recognize that there is a lot more to your youth ministry than simply what you see on the surface of any program. There is a goal behind each of the programs your youth ministry offers. As you begin to identify each program's purposes, you'll understand better how you can help fulfill the purposes and contribute to the team. If you don't know the purpose of a program...please ask. It's not a secret. If you're a leader, you need to be informed so you can be supportive.

when leadership and friendship collide

Being a leader among your friends is tough, especially when they aren't leaders. When your buddy starts messing around in the middle of a Bible study, it's very tempting to join in and flick popcorn into that old lady's big hair. Not only is it funny, it's also enjoyable to mess around when you're not supposed to. But being a student leader requires you to live by a higher standard. Plus, you're part of a team, and the actions of leaders should support other leaders.

If you want to be a friend and a leader, you'll need to draw some clear lines so you and your friends know when it's time to lead and when it's time to goof off. You'll be required to establish some commitments and stick to them even when they're tough to keep (and usually, they are hard to keep when breaking them involves friends). Here are two commitments I suggest you consider making.

• **Commit to protecting the ministry.** The student leader is expected to play a part on the leadership team that strengthens the ministry. If your friends are doing anything that undermines the health of the ministry, you need to move away from that action and speak out in love about their behavior. In those rare moments, it's time to be a leader and speak to that friend who is disrespectful, divisive, or causing problems. You'll need to speak and act in a way that shows you care about your friend but that you're also concerned about the ministry and want to protect it from potentially harmful actions.

• **Commit to developing relationships.** You've learned already that one of your key responsibilities as a leader is to serve others. If your friends aren't leaders, they may not carry that same burden. They may be only consumers of the ministry who enjoy hanging out in a place that is both comfortable and safe. That's okay for them...but not for you. As a student leader you can't ignore the needs of others.

If your friends choose to overlook the lonely or the visitors, that's their option. You don't have that option. You've made a commitment to serve, and one of the major ways you do that is by caring for others. This tension over different commitments will provide you with a great opportunity to hold less tightly to your friends or clique and be a model to them of what a student leader does. You'll be surprised at the respect you'll receive when you commit to serve God through serving others. One of our current student leaders, Curtis, became more committed to Christ, to church, and to others because his buddy Dominic was such a great example of a committed student leader. It's amazing how attractive commitment is to those who aren't committed.

When you're determined to keep these leadership commitments, you'll find them guiding you and helping you maintain and perhaps redefine your friendships. Again, it's not easy being a student leader in a youth group when your friends aren't as committed as you are. You're not alone in experiencing this tension. Most leaders struggle to balance leadership commitments with belonging to a group of friends who don't lead others. You may find yourself backing away from some of your friendships in order to commit to relationships with other leaders and to the roles and responsibilities that come with leading. Being a leader isn't easy...but it will be rewarding as you learn the balance of friendship and leadership. You can do it!

when it's bad...go positive

The year it rained on our spring break mission trip to Mexico was another memorable experience. We were flooded out of our campground. It was the first time this had happened to me in more than 25 years of taking trips. And since we knew it "never rains on our Mexico trip," we hadn't made alternate plans in case it rained.

The camp was a total disaster! Tents blew away, sound equipment was ruined, and we scrambled to figure out how and where to move students and volunteers before we all drowned. We needed dry blankets to replace drenched sleeping bags, and all the stores were closed—making all this an even greater challenge. I look back on this trip as both a costly disaster and an awesome memory. Now I count it as one of my favorite trips ever.

What made this disastrous trip so great were miracles from God and positive attitudes from our student leaders. A few whiners spreading a negative attitude through the camp was all it would have taken to replace my positive memory with a painful one.

When circumstances get beyond human control, one proof you're being a good student leader is how you respond to difficult situations. Read the following questions and decide how you might react to each:

• Are you a team player who's willing to support a plan you may not agree with?

• **Do you withdraw and secretly hope for others to fail?**
• **Do you complain and damage the morale of the group?**

If you answered "yes" to the first question, that's good. Being a team player is the only healthy way to respond to a difficult situation. Even if you don't like what's going on, maintaining a positive attitude and being helpful will give you leadership credibility. Leaders are known for how they react to adverse situations, not for their ability to be in the spotlight. When problems arise (and they will), view them as opportunities to prove your dedication to the team and as chances to demonstrate your sincere desire to be a servant leader.

Here are some ways my student leaders helped make life easier during our Mexico disaster:

• **Moving luggage**
• **Keeping the shelter clean**
• **Working to save the sound equipment**
• **Solving minor problems on their own**
• **Sharing dry clothes**
• **Distributing blankets**
• **Not complaining (This was a biggie!)**

All their help and positive attitudes caused the other students to follow their examples. I can't imagine how much worse the situation would have been without their help. Because they made right choices, every need was met, the trip became a successful memory, and my student leaders enhanced their value to the ministry team.

I challenge you to always be positive about what's going on in a program or at an event. I hope you'll never be part of an event like our Mexico trip. Still, make a commitment right now to be positive (no matter what happens), and you'll be better prepared for the times when ministry gets crazy.

Hey, good job...thank you

As a youth pastor, one of my favorite moments is observing other leaders encouraging one another. I love it! I'm feeling excitement even as I write this section. (And it's rare for me to be excited to write. I'd rather be kicked in the head!) Let me tell you why I'm excited. Typically, most people are torn down verbally and ridiculed for small, everyday mistakes. I'm referring to those easy, daily opportunities we find to sarcastically tease and embarrass others. It's so rare to hear people offer encouraging comments. As a leader please make a commitment to be different and develop the habit of encouraging other leaders.

Jesus said, "Your love for one another will prove to the world that you are my disciples" (John 13:35, NLT). Jesus' words imply, "They'll know you are a group of hypocrites if you treat one another poorly, and they'll know there's something different about you when you speak words of encouragement."

Over the years I've been disappointed and felt unsupported or not encouraged in my leadership efforts hundreds of times. Often a simple "thank you" from another leader has made a huge difference in my life. Typically, I can last another week when someone says something positive about my leadership or my ministry contribution. Encouragement is a powerful leadership tool, and it's easy to do. Just say, "Thanks." A kind word lets me know I'm not alone and that someone on the team is in my corner, cheering me on.

What are some simple ways you can provide encouragement to other leaders in your church? Spend some time answering this question and discussing it with other leaders. Soon kind words will appear on your mental and verbal radar screens. But while encouragement is easy, it won't happen automatically. Here are some ideas to get you started:

- **When you notice something positive about a person's action, comment on it.** Let other leaders know when you see them do something worthy of encouragement.

- **Jump in to help.** Offering unsolicited help bonds leaders together and acts as a source of encouragement.

- **Stop gossip.** When you hear gossip and stop it, you'll end problems before they appear and show you value other team members.

- **Speak highly of people behind their backs.** When

you do this, you'll create an atmosphere where people won't complain about their leaders because they'll know all the leaders are supporting one another. When you speak in negative terms about other leaders, you invite everyone's opinion and criticism. Stay clear of that mess.

• **Be dependable.** If you make a commitment, keep it without having to be reminded. Arrive early at an event and stay late. If you can't keep a commitment, let other leaders know ASAP.

Why don't you be the type of leader to start this trend? Don't wait for someone else to read this book to get the encouragement started. You may notice that nowhere in this section do I reference student leaders only. All leaders need encouragement! The adult leaders, your pastor, and your peers need your good words. Providing encouragement will make ministry and leadership more enjoyable, and the church's leaders will be much more productive when all involved aren't focused on themselves.

when you don't agree

You'll discover this about leadership sooner or later, so I might as well let you in on it sooner: Being a leader will bring you some pain. Pain comes with the leadership territory. Conflict and leadership go hand in hand. But if you learn to navigate the waves of disagreement effectively, you'll learn an essential survival skill necessary for all leaders.

Most student leaders panic during times of conflict. They feel awkward, tense, confused, and fearful about conflict with others. Many leaders try to avoid the tension. That's the popular method of denial. Either people pretend the conflict doesn't exist or that it will go away eventually. Denial describes my conflict management style when I was a young leader. I'd experience the tension of the conflict, retreat, and pout in private. While it was easy to deny the conflict, it never proved helpful in resolving it.

As a leader you must learn to face your conflicts and pursue peace. Let's say the lead youth worker at your church decides to cancel an event you love. You're angry, right? You don't think it was a good decision. So, what do you do when you don't agree with her decision? Well, you probably shouldn't cuss, kick a puppy, or go screaming into the church office and call the leader a communist. But you also don't want to live in denial, pretend everything's fine, and wait for the tension to go away (which it won't). Instead I suggest you ask yourself the following questions:

1. Why do I think the decision was made?
2. What positive comments can I make about the decision?
3. What good might result because of the decision?
4. What do I hope happens as a result of the decision?
5. Why do I feel so strongly about the decision?

Write down your answers to these questions and then set them aside for a few hours. Later, reread your answers and adjust them to reflect any new thoughts you've had since answering the questions originally.

Now you need to decide how to respond to the decision you disagree with. Here are some options:

• **Accept her decision and support it.** Even if you don't agree with the decision, you need to be a leader and team player—which means you support leadership decisions. (Side note: You may not be privileged to know all the reasons behind a decision. Students have been angry with me for a decision even when they knew nothing of all the prayer, conversations with others, and wisdom seeking I pursued prior to making the decision. They were angry they didn't get their way and assumed I made a bad decision without prayer and guidance. Please know that most leaders don't make important decisions without praying, talking to others about them, or asking important questions.)

• **Make a list of suggestions and alternatives you believe would improve the decision.** Express these thoughts to the decision maker.

• **Get out of the way.** If you cannot support the decision, I encourage you to remove yourself from being an obstacle. This may mean not participating in the event or, in extreme situations, stepping away from student leadership. If you can't be supportive, you'll be divisive.

Whatever you decide, being divisive, gossiping, and responding with rage are not acceptable or biblical options for a leader. If you learn how to manage conflict at a young age, you'll be more prepared for the bigger conflicts coming your way. If you lead, conflict will follow!

If you don't support the ministry through your actions, conversations, and participation, you're not building up the ministry. In my youth ministry I've asked some student leaders to step away from being leaders until they're able to better hold to this commitment. If the time comes when they believe they're ready to dedicate themselves to support the ministry, we'll discuss the expectations of the leadership role and see if they are ones the students can handle. If this describes you, you'll have more integrity stepping down from a leadership position than you will if you claim to be a leader but don't support the other leaders.

Hold onto your ideas...loosely

I hope that as a result of reading this chapter you understand better what's going on in your ministry and how you can support other leaders. As you seek to understand the big picture of your youth ministry, you'll devise a few ideas you'd like to see take shape. Pray about these ideas and set up a meeting to share them with your youth leader. But hold your ideas with a loose grip—be willing to let them go if they're not accepted.

Before you go into the meeting, ask God to use you and your ideas to make a positive impact on the youth ministry. But don't be too discouraged if your ideas are not adopted immediately. If they're rejected— for whatever reason—you've joined a huge team of other leaders who've left their ideas at the feet of the main leader. But if your ideas are adopted, congratulations! Whatever happens, generating ideas and presenting them in a caring and sensitive manner will make a positive contribution to the team.

Taking a loose-grip approach to your ideas allows your leader to evaluate whether or not the ideas will work with the current vision for the ministry. If you have a loose grip on the ideas, and they're not adopted, you'll learn something about your motives. If you react to the rejection with anger, you'll know you may have a pride issue that you need to address. If you react with genuine willingness to adopt the direction your leader chooses, you'll know you're developing maturity as a student leader.

Your job as a student leader isn't to change the ministry—it's to serve it, understand it, and support it.

A last leadership thought and challenge

There's a lot to learn in this chapter, and I know you're the type of leader who'll consume this material and put it into practice. My challenge for you is to seek to understand the purpose behind all your youth ministry programs. Write down the name of each program and then write down what you believe are the primary biblical purposes of each program—these might include discipleship, fellowship, ministry, worship, or evangelism. If you don't know, ask! This will be a good exercise for you and the other student leaders who are reading this book.

Alyssa's Notes

Supporting the ministry and other leaders is an area of strength for me. I understand the purpose of our events and why we do the things we do, and that means I'm better able to speak positively to complaining students and support our leaders. The results have been immediate and positive, so I try really hard to be supportive of our youth ministry at all times. Remember: People will listen to you and take into account what you say. Even helping one person to understand and become more supportive of the ministry really can make a difference.

Chapter Five

Student Leaders Solve Problems

In the last chapter you learned you're not living alone in your leadership world. You're part of a team, and your actions either enhance or diminish the effectiveness of the ministry. This chapter closely associates itself with the concept of teamwork because when you learn to solve problems on your own, you'll contribute to the health and strength of the team. Typically student leaders drag other student leaders into their issues and conflicts. This results in a lot of wasted time and personal energy.

As you read this chapter, keep in mind that you're part of a bigger team, and if the problem ever gets too much for you to deal with, don't hesitate to ask for help. But when you begin to think like a problem solver, you'll be amazed at what you can handle successfully on your own.

Be part of the solution

As a leader, either the severity of the need or the level of your leadership determines how you respond to a need. Sadly, I've watched student leaders wait to respond to problems until they've become too severe for one person to

deal with. "The guy is bleeding all over the youth room...
I should do something." Anyone can identify obvious
needs, but not everyone has the leadership awareness to
see a need and meet it without being asked. I want you to
learn to meet needs without being asked. I want you to
learn to meet needs before they whirl out of control.

By taking this initiative, you will increase your
leadership skills, and your significance to the team will
take another step forward. This concept is a biggie to
grasp. You really only have three potential responses to
needs—ignore them, report them, or take care of them:

• **Ignore needs.** I hope this is not the option you
choose. When you ignore needs, the health of the
ministry suffers.

• **Report needs.** If reporting needs is all you do, you
may be creating stress for others on your team.
Reporting a need is only acceptable when you or
other student leaders aren't capable of meeting it on
your own. Anyone can report a need. For example,
"Hey, Doug, we need to set up more chairs." That
report isn't helpful to anyone. I want a leader to do
something more.

• **Take care of needs.** Make this your automatic
response. For instance, if more chairs need to be
set up, make it happen instead of telling someone
about the problem. Or if you see someone standing
by himself, don't point him out to your leader

and say, "Look, Doug, there's a visitor." Instead introduce yourself and invite the person into your group of friends.

If you see a need and choose to report it instead of taking care of it, you're missing a great opportunity to be a leader. Often I say to my student leaders, "Will you please see if you can figure out a solution to that problem?" Guess what? The majority of the time, they do. They're awesome leaders who haven't figured out how capable they really are.

Typically, most needs you believe at first are worthy of reporting are needs you can handle on your own with a little thought and attention. For example, if you see students juggling snakes in the bathroom, say something. If you find yourself getting into a situation bigger than you're capable of handling (the snakes are actually eating small children), then it's time to ask for help. (I tell my student leaders that if another student is threatening a life, another or his own, I want to know about it immediately. I don't want them to try to solve that type of problem alone.)

But in most cases I'd rather you attempt to solve problems and make mistakes than not try at all. Actually, there aren't many mistakes that can't be fixed or explained away. If you're going to make a mistake, make sure it's a good one. It's better to make a big mistake because of enthusiasm for leadership and conviction of belief than not to do anything at all. If you have a question, say something such as, "Doug, I really want to solve this problem on my own, but I want to make sure you're okay with my leadership on this particular issue. If you are, I'll go for it. If you're not, I'll give you the details, and I'll step away." By doing this, you're communicating that you want to take the lead, but you're a little unsure if you can handle the problem. I appreciate honesty when a leader isn't sure.

Leaders take ownership for their ministry and look for opportunities to meet needs without running to an adult to solve the problem. When you do this, you'll find yourself developing new leadership skills and gaining respect from other leaders. Okay? Next time, go for it!

Keep short accounts

As I mention in Chapter Four, conflict is connected to leadership. Wherever people are, there will be tension. "Keep short accounts" is a challenge to solve relationship conflict as soon as possible so the *accounts* don't get overdrawn, causing more tension and conflict.

When conflict isn't resolved in a timely manner, it causes hard feelings and creates division in your ministry. But when conflict is handled quickly and correctly, it brings people closer together and strengthens your ministry. This is another time where I would lean close to you at our fast-food restaurant meeting and say very firmly, "If you want to be an effective leader, you must learn to deal with relational conflict. There's no getting around this one. Resolving conflict is part of leadership."

For me, when conflict hits, I need to quiet myself, pray, and seek God's wisdom before I approach the other person and seek peaceful restoration.

I've learned a lot about what to do (and not to do) when others are upset with me. Here are a few tips:

• **Don't avoid the person.** People who store up their anger will spew it out eventually. When this happens, a person may say things with more emotion than reason. Don't give her the opportunity to collect verbal ammunition. If you know someone is upset with you, consider approaching her to deal with it. A short battle is less damaging than a long war. I might say something like this to the person: "I've had the impression there's some tension between us. If so, I'd be happy to talk about it."

• **Listen until she's finished.** Good communication requires you allow others to share fully how they're feeling without interrupting. You'll be tempted to interrupt in an attempt to be defensive or to clarify. But let her speak, and then it will be your turn to respond once you've heard everything clearly. Plus, this is an honoring way to treat people.

• **Don't attack.** Avoid offensive language (such as using the word *you*) and the temptation to be defensive (which usually leads to attacking back). You may find this difficult to do, but healthy communication needs to be void of personal attacks.

- **End with positive comments.** Almost always I end a conflict on a positive note. In a relational conflict I want the person to leave feeling that she has been heard and understood. I want her to know her input is appreciated and that the door is left open for future communication.

Now you might be thinking, "Well, what about when I'm upset with others?" That's an excellent question—you're such a good leader. Here are a few more tips.

- **Be careful to avoid division.** Don't attempt to bring others to your side of the conflict. If they're not part of the problem or the solution, don't share the conflict with them and get them involved.

- **Go to the source.** When I've tried to resolve conflicts through third parties, I've always messed it up. Most tension begins with a misunderstanding that gets blown into a frenzy by an overactive imagination, rumor, or gossip. Cut it off quickly and clearly by going straight to the source.

- **Walk in his shoes.** Many problems happen because of circumstances I don't understand. It took me several years to learn a simple principle of conflict management: There are two sides to every story. Because I know why I'm upset, I often assume I know the solution without considering other people's feelings. However, when I look beyond my anger and consider the other's point of view, I see his perspective (even if I don't agree with him). If you do this, it'll help calm you down and be less offensive when you speak to other people.

- **Seek wise counsel.** On the surface this action may appear to be the opposite advice from "Go to the source." When I seek counsel, I'm not trying to get someone to resolve the conflict for me; rather I want to bounce the situation off of someone I respect. You can do this carefully by speaking in generalities and by keeping the discussion away from gossip. Typically when I do this, I seek counsel from someone who doesn't know the other person involved in the conflict.

- **Speak the truth carefully.** When I'm ready to talk to the person about the conflict, I must do so in a way that's not offensive. I'll always confront the issue in private—always praise in public and confront in private. I'll be careful to keep a sharp watch on my attitude, my nonverbal communication, and my words. I'll speak in a tender and nonthreatening tone. Often I'll start the conversation by apologizing, taking ownership for my part in the conflict, and asking forgiveness for the role I played. When that's done, the other person isn't defensive and we're able to address the issues.

When you keep short accounts…

…conflict and its resolution become strengthening factors in your relationships.

…you'll be relieved of the stress that comes from bottling up anger or frustration.

…you'll develop skills needed to handle future disagreements.

You can't be a leader and escape conflict. So you've either got to stop leading or figure out how to deal with it. (I know what you'll choose to do, and I'm proud of you for making the right choice!)

Arguing without being defensive

Recently one of my student leaders asked me if it was possible to defend her ideas without sounding defensive. After some discussion we decided it was possible but very difficult. Most of the time we get too defensive while arguing our points, and we create additional conflicts. Basically we decided that defensiveness is arguing without trying to understand the other side. We sat down and discussed some ways we could become better listeners, communicators, and problem solvers without being defensive. Here are a few of our ideas:

• **Before you defend your position...take notes.** While it's very tempting, don't begin formulating your response to the other person while she's talking. Otherwise you may get stuck on a comment and either interrupt her or stop listening altogether. This is a learned listening skill. If it's helpful (and if you have a pen), jot down a key word she said or one you thought of as you continue to listen. By doing this you won't forget what you want to say when it's your turn to talk.

• **Ask clarifying questions.** When a person knows you genuinely want to understand his position, he may become less intense. Also, by getting him to dialogue with you about his side of the argument, he may see something he hadn't considered previously. Talking through issues calmly and respectfully has a powerful effect on your ability to think and argue rationally.

• **Point out similarities.** What do you agree on? Do you ultimately share the same goal but go down different roads to get there? Often we may disagree on the method of getting something done, but we have the same goal. Arguments are easier to end when we realize how much we agree on the goal.

• **Consider a compromise.** The ability to compromise shows you value the other person's point of view and want to diffuse the tension. As both of you lower your defenses, almost always you'll be able to reach a decision to join forces, create a new plan, or merge your ideas together.

Defensiveness will escalate conflict; a calm and thoughtful approach will deflate anger. Defensiveness triggers pride and determination; understanding encourages compromise.

Developing these leadership and conflict-management skills will not only improve your ministry, but will also help you better handle conflict in every area of life…at home, school, work, college, and in your future marriage and career. Conflict is unavoidable. It's everywhere…the sooner you learn to manage it, the better off you'll be.

I guarantee you'll make mistakes in dealing with conflict. I've taught thousands of adult ministers how to resolve conflict, and we tell stories of how we continue to mess up. The next time you mess up, reread this section and determine what you could have done better in your handling of the relationship. The art of defending your position without being defensive will help you succeed where most people fail.

Stop rumors

Most people love a good rumor. We are rumor-hungry people who feed off gossip and support multimillion-dollar gossip companies by purchasing magazines and newspapers that nourish our appetite for other people's business. This love for gossip leaks into the church every single day.

Rumors are often bits of information overheard, passed on by others, and embellished from one person to the next. Usually there is little truth in a rumor and a lot of inaccurate information. The further the truth moves away from its original source, the less accurate it is. Eventually a rumor loses all resemblance to the truth.

How do your ears react to gossip? Are you capable of turning away when you hear it? You may not even realize you're spreading rumors because talking about others feels so natural. Unfortunately, the bad news about rumors is that they are a symptom of a heart distant from God. Rumors destroy a healthy life and ministry. I challenge you to stop spreading them and listening to them. Here are a few suggestions that may help you deal with the ugliness of rumors:

• **Dispel the rumor by sharing the truth.** If you know the truth behind the rumor, either you can share it (if it's not confidential), or you can say, "You don't have the correct information, and you shouldn't be talking about that situation."

• **Invite the subject of the rumor into the conversation.** If the person who is the subject of the rumor is nearby, invite him into the conversation to talk about what is being said about him (this is the best way to stop a rumor). For example, if Kyle wants to tell me a rumor about Shaun, I'd say, "Hey, Shaun, come here for a minute. Kyle is telling me something about you." You'll be amazed at how quickly Kyle closes his mouth.

• **Change the subject.** If you're in a conversation and a rumor comes up, you can say, "We shouldn't be talking about that because I'm not part of the problem or the solution." Abrupt? Yes. Helpful? Absolutely! When someone said this to me, three things happened: I shut up, I had a new level of respect for the person who said it, and I learned what to do the next time someone attempts to gossip.

Learn to ask the question, "Am I part of the problem or the solution?" If the answer is no, then you have no business discussing the situation.

The bad news about rumors is that they don't build others up. One of the main roles of being a leader is to build others up and honor God with your life. Listening to rumors doesn't belong in the life of a leader. If you earn a reputation for spreading rumors, your effectiveness as a leader will diminish. You'll lose the respect of others and friendships, and your problems will increase. I learned how to deal with rumors the hard way. And here's what I learned: When in doubt, shut up.

Is the conflict worth it?

Within every conflict is an opportunity to tear down or build up another person. The way you choose to deal with conflict will determine your effectiveness as a leader. Because life is filled with conflicts, you'll have many opportunities to refine your conflict-resolution skills.

But before you choose to respond to a conflict, consider spending time deciding if the conflict is worth your energy. Are you passionate about the issue? Honestly, many potential conflicts are not worth your time. If you addressed everything you didn't like, you would not only receive a reputation as a whiner, but you'd also be very busy being disappointed.

If you decide an issue is worth your attention, you'll want to consider how best to respond. The way you choose to deal with conflict is just as important as deciding which conflicts you'll address. For example, let's say you use a hammer to kill a mosquito on your friend's arm. While it would be funny and make a great video, your friend will be angrier about your problem-solving method than the mosquito bite.

Here's an example of a conflict I didn't think was worth entering into: Today a publisher presented me with eight options for a book cover (not for this book), and I didn't love any of them. This was the third round of book covers I'd seen. Because of what's going on in my life right now (a bunch of details to deal with, people, ministry, finishing this book, etc.), I had to determine whether the potential conflict with the artist was worth it. I decided it wasn't. I've written several books, and I've learned that while covers are very important, it's the content that makes a great book. Because of this I chose a cover I really liked rather than fight for a new one in the hope that I'd love it. This saved me from a conflict I didn't really need.

I encourage you to learn when to fight for the biggies and let the little ones go. This decision will require you to beg God for his wisdom. Conflict is everywhere, but not every conflict is worth your time and effort.

A last leadership thought and challenge

I encourage you to choose to deal with your conflicts in an honest, God-honoring way. Seek to resolve conflict in a face-to-face setting. Don't rush into resolving the conflict. Withdrawing from the situation gives you time to think. Then you can reengage with the person in a calm manner at a later time. The problem with other communication methods (e-mail, phone, answering machine, etc.) is that you cannot "un-hit" the send button on an e-mail or take back a message on an answering machine or change your vocal tone over the phone once you cool down. When you handle a conflict in person, words are chosen more carefully, and nonverbal communication (body language) helps enhance what you may have trouble putting into words (e.g., a hug, a tearful eye, caring facial expressions, etc).

You'll have plenty of opportunities to develop these communication skills and solve problems in the future. But why don't you look for an opportunity to put one of these actions into practice this week? Who is someone in your life with whom you're experiencing tension? Based on what you've read in this chapter, what can you do to seek a peaceful resolution to the conflict with this person?

Alyssa's Notes

I think church is unfortunately one of the worst environments when it comes to gossip. This really bothers me, and I have thought about it a great deal. The old rule of only talking about the issue if you are a part of the problem or the solution can fail us at times. One of the problems I have been guilty of and have observed in other student leaders is that we start thinking we can be a part of EVERY solution. We may be able to help sometimes, but this excuse quickly turns into a justification of gossip. Doug's clear advice in this chapter encourages me to stop trying to become a part of every solution and to start defeating gossip.

Chapter Six

Student Leaders Have a Ministry

You're definitely unique!

Have you ever worked hard to make something and then watched it be destroyed before you ever got to use it? This happened to me when I was 12 years old. I made a very nice switchblade knife out of popsicle sticks and rubber bands. As I was crafting it, my friends commented on my creation with envy. They placed orders for me to make them some. Unfortunately, the unthinkable happened when I left my creation on the kitchen table. Our dog Lucy sniffed the sugary scent left on the sticks and chewed my masterpiece apart. I was very disappointed. I hated Lucy for several days until I had to pick up her mess in the backyard. I noticed some wood from the sticks in it. I laughed and thought, "That must have hurt." Delayed revenge...it felt good (for me, not for Lucy).

Much like my disappointment, I imagine the creator God also experiences pain when his designs aren't used the way he intended. God made you exactly how he wanted you. He created you to love, worship, and serve while serving others.

Consider how God's wired you. He gave you a unique heart that loves things others don't love. For example, I love sports...my wife doesn't. But she loves music...and I don't. That's great! We love different things—that's how God wired us. And you, too. God gave all of us different abilities. You don't have the same skills as your best friend and vice versa. Think about your personality—so different from others. I have three children, and they have very different personalities even though they come from the same parents. What's up with that? When you take your loves, your abilities, and your personality and bundle them into the unique experiences you've already had in life...you are an original masterpiece. There's no one like you! I hope that makes you feel great. God thinks you are one of a kind and doesn't want anyone else in the world to be exactly like you.

When you realize God's unique fingerprints are all over your life, you can seek to discover what it is God wants you to do in this world. Since you're an original masterpiece, there's a ministry waiting for you that will use the winning combination of your spiritual gifts, your heart, your abilities, your personality, and your experiences.

What might that ministry be? A growing leader is required to discover how uniquely she's created and to discover how God wants to use her uniqueness to serve him. When you discover God's plan, you'll be thrilled, and you'll feel like you're doing exactly what God wants you to do.

As I said, I'm not a big music fan (I like music, but I don't love it). I have no musical abilities. I'm an extrovert, and I have a lot of experience living in large suburbs close to cities. Because I have these traits and experiences, my ministry will never be teaching guitar lessons to one person living in Amish country. But someone needs to have a music ministry to our Amish friends. It's just not me.

Set out on a leadership journey to discover how God shaped you uniquely and how that unique shape might best prepare you for a personalized ministry. You're created for a great purpose—discover it, turn it into your ministry, and you'll fulfill God's purpose for you.

I believe ministry fulfillment can happen for you right now. Yes, even as a teenager. You don't have to wait until you're an adult to have a ministry to others. You can serve God and others right now. This might not be the ministry you do for the rest of your life, but you (as a student leader) can and should have a ministry today. Keep reading and begin asking God where you might be used.

Be contagious

When you serve in a ministry and make a commitment to discover your unique, God-given shape, you'll become a contagious Christian. And you'll use that wonderful discovery to guide others toward some type of ministry. They'll want to be involved in ministry when they see you in action.

If you've felt frustrated when trying to get others involved in a ministry, you're not alone. This frustration finds me all the time. When you set out to make others into ministers, you may find you run into a fear of failure. Like me, you'll be rejected in your efforts to involve other people in ministry.

When others are involved in a ministry, they'll grow spiritually, the church will be strengthened, and God will honor you for encouraging the involvement of others. Others need to know they're important to God, too. They need to understand they have gifts and are called to serve God in some manner as well. By helping to involve your friends in ministry, you'll help them see that their contributions will ultimately benefit the body of Christ.

Everybody feels the need to experience significance. No one wants to merely take up space on this planet. Knowing you're doing something to make a difference in the world is a powerful and rewarding feeling. So when you get others involved in a ministry, you're helping them belong to something, contribute to something, and feel good about themselves. When a person's need to belong is met, he'll feel more alive and more open to going deeper in a relationship with God.

Here are some things I've learned about trying to get others involved in serving in a ministry:

1. Usually other people are concerned more about themselves than anything else.
2. Other people want to belong and feel needed.
3. Other people are capable of having passion for meeting a need.
4. Other people don't want to be tricked or pushed

into helping. They'd rather do it because they want to.

It's important to understand what's happening inside a person's mind if you're going to help with his involvement in ministry. Here are some further descriptions of different attitudes you'll encounter as you try to involve others in ministry:

- **Self-centeredness.** Because you understand that people are self-centered by nature, you'll need to think about how they'll benefit from being involved in a ministry. Think about how each person is shaped and gifted by God. Think about what he'll get out of serving in a particular ministry. Be sure to hand out plenty of encouragement and praise—that becomes the positive fuel for those of us who are self-centered.

- **The need to belong.** Typically a person needs an invitation to become involved in a ministry. This person is like a piece of ripe fruit waiting to be picked off a tree. If he hangs there too long, he'll fall off the tree, rot, and be worthless. But if he's picked in time, he'll be a great person to serve in a ministry. Anyone alone and unconnected to others is ripe for an invitation to serve.

- **Awaken the passion.** If a person isn't passionate about helping, either he won't get involved or won't do a good job. The best way to discover someone's passion is to ask questions and listen for an excited response. When someone talks enough, his passion will leak out in the conversation. Listen carefully for clues to the passion, identify it, and point the person to a ministry where the passion will be used. As a leader you need to watch for ways to align ministry opportunities with people's passions. When you're talking with a friend and discover her passion is video, help her start a video ministry or get involved with an existing one.

- **People don't like pushy.** Think about your own family. The harder your parents push you to do something, the less happy you are to do it. This isn't tough to understand. Most people don't like to be pushed into doing anything. Never use the words, "Will you do _____ for me?" "For me" is a subtle way to elevate you above them. When it seems you'll become their supervisor, they'll be less likely to get involved. After all, it's not about what they can do for you; it's really about helping them get in the game and experience the joy of serving God.

I want all students to graduate high school with some type of ministry experience. When a youth group graduates ministers, it is a healthy ministry. Please don't allow all the promoting, recruiting, and placement of ministers to fall on the lead youth worker. When you're excited about ministry, your peers will be excited, too. When you're together with your friends, talk about ministry opportunities and dream about making a difference in the world through serving God. When you get excited about ministry, your excitement will be contagious to those around you.

Think globally

Because you're reading this book, I'm assuming you're richer than about two thirds of the people in the world. Most people will never know what it's like to be able to buy a book and afford some of the other simple luxuries you've grown accustomed to.

Because you have more wealth than most of the world, you have something to offer others. In addition to wealth, you have access to the richest news in the world, the good news of God's love for creation, to share with others. Don't limit your thinking to what you read in this chapter; instead begin to dream big dreams. Student leaders need to develop a global mindset. Here are some ways you might begin thinking about ministry opportunities outside your church:

• **Find a good cause and partner with someone to work for it.** Your youth ministry can align itself with several organizations that can help expose those in your ministry to global ministry opportunities. For example, our youth group is involved with several partners. We sponsor poor children in partnership with an international mission. We also help finance an AIDS ministry to Africa, and we participate in a fundraiser sponsored by an international relief organization to raise money to feed people in poor countries. There are hundreds of mission organizations out there. All you need to do is start looking.

• **Create options for student involvement.** Not every student will be ready to make a global impact. But your job as a leader is to create different ways to expose others to the big causes. For example, not every person is ready to go on a mission trip, but some might take a first step by helping with a car wash designed to raise money for your mission trip. Get others involved in seeing needs around the world.

• **Go global.** Many youth ministries take students on trips to other countries to help struggling churches. Your church can do this, too. Do it on your own, partner with another church, or sign up to go as part of a global mission's organization. I spoke with some teenagers from our church who traveled to Brazil to help a needy church, and they went without me (their youth pastor). I went on the first trip, and now other trips happen without me. Every time our students return from an international mission trip, I see *changed life* written all over their faces.

If your youth ministry hasn't done a mission trip before, I recommend partnering with your denomination, another church, or a mission organization that has some prior mission experience. A mission trip is not a good activity to learn how to do by trial and error. In order to be successful, I go with an experienced group first.

This chapter is not an attempt to guilt you into selling everything you own and sending your money to a hungry child in Africa. Rather I want you to think big—and I mean big, as in impossible big. It sounds goofy, but I'm talking about something so big it would be impossible to do without God's help. Don't let anything limit your thinking about what God may want to do through you and your youth ministry. Consider this verse as you dream big: "Jesus looked at them intently and said, 'Humanly speaking, it is impossible. But not with God. Everything is possible with God'" (Mark 10:27, NLT). Open your eyes to the needs in the world and set your mind in a global direction.

Make contact

Before you finish this chapter, let me suggest a ministry that doesn't require you to think big. Actually, the idea is really simple. It's an entry-level ministry opportunity I believe all student leaders should participate in along with their other acts of service. Ready? Think small. Postage stamp small.

Send letters or make phone calls.

Everybody loves getting personal mail, and most people appreciate receiving a "How are you?" phone call. You can't imagine how excited someone might be if you took the time to make a personal connection in one of those two ways. I know this is a simple idea, but all student leaders should make it a priority to contact their peers within their youth ministry.

Too often the task of calling and following up with attendees is left to the youth pastor. But let's be honest—it's really not that special when a youth pastor calls or writes a member of the youth group. After all, many of us are the age of your parents. But when a note or phone call comes from a peer, it can be very special.

So even if you're using your gifts in another ministry, I encourage you to begin a ministry of follow-up or participate in it if it already exists. This includes contacting the visitors, calling those who haven't been to church in a while, and letting other regular attendees know there are student leaders who care and want to make sure the students are connected and doing okay.

Contacting another person represents concern. The method of contact doesn't matter as much as the fact that you make a personal contact. The more personal the contact, the better and the more it will have a lasting impact on the person. Please don't write, "Our records reflect you've been missing from Sunday school." Instead make a note or phone call unique to the individual: "I haven't seen you in a while, Tiffany, and I was wondering if everything is okay or if there's anything I can pray about for you." If that feels too uncomfortable, call with a specific reason in mind. For example, say, "I was calling to tell you we're having camp sign-up this weekend. I wanted to make sure you knew about it. By the way, how's it going?"

These types of contacts will make a difference in students' lives. Following up with students should be a significant task in a student leader's ministry. Some teenagers have a lot of hidden hurt feelings of insignificance and self-doubt. These can be minimized and even erased when you go out of your way to make personal connections with others. You may never know how much you helped that person, but the action you take will make a big difference. It did with me!

A last leadership thought and challenge

If you were in my youth ministry, I'd be thrilled to consider you a student leader. But being a student leader wouldn't be enough—I want you to be a student leader who has a ministry. It can be anything. You can be a greeter. You can lead singing. You can teach Sunday school. You can lead a Bible study on your campus. You can do graphic design for the church bulletin. You could try to teach four-year-olds how to do their own baptisms. (Okay, I'm kidding.) Really, I wouldn't care what you did as long as your motives were right. I hope that behind your ministry there is a desire to serve God based on your unique heart, skills, personality, and the needs you see—big needs and huge needs. If you graduate high school with a minister's heart and vision, you'll be dangerous for God's kingdom and tick off the enemy. I challenge you to get involved in a ministry ASAP. If you're already involved in one, try to get some of your friends participating in a ministry. When you begin to minister, you'll never be the same.

Alyssa's Notes

I went to Brazil this summer, and my life was completely changed. My ideas about church, God, servanthood, joy, peace, and many other things were completely redefined. More specifically, God showed me that I was trying to put all of those things in a little box. God replaced these notions with much larger pictures, and I still don't even come close to understanding it all. As student leaders we need to be careful not to get so wrapped up in the motions of church, leading, serving in a ministry, etc., that we forget how big God is. Just as Doug suggested, by getting involved, praying, and being active in some way around the world, we really can be reminded of how big God is.

Chapter Seven

Student Leaders Focus on Their Own Families

I love talking to the parents of the kids in my youth group and bragging about what I see their kids doing. I want moms and dads to feel a healthy pride in having their children involved in the youth ministry and in their kid's spiritual growth. Often parents are surprised to hear these comments about their kids. They'll tell me I must have their child confused with someone else. Their lame attempt at humor tells me that many youth group students live double lives. They behave one way at home and show other behavior at church events.

I hate hearing stories about some of our student leaders who seem to be stars at church and disrespectful at home. I find it odd how someone can be helpful, caring, and compassionate at church activities and then act in a different way completely when away from the youth ministry. I realize that everyone goes through teenage issues that can make parents crazy, but my hope is that a student leader will make her home life as healthy as her church life.

Right now imagine your parents bragging to your youth pastor about how great you are at home. Now that would be a fun switch! This chapter is about helping to make that a reality.

Influence up

I want to introduce you to a principle known as *upward influence*. It describes what can happen when something seen as weaker enhances something seen as stronger. For example, a minimum wage worker at a fast-food restaurant (a weak person in terms of power) can have upward influence on the franchise owner (a strong person in terms of power) by working hard and showing a cheerful attitude. If the owner becomes more cheerful, upward influence has occurred.

Upward influence can change your family dynamics over time. When you change who you are at home, you'll influence your family to change. But changing your image at home won't happen overnight. Your family has developed an understanding of your character over a long time. Positively changing that perception will take more time. For example, if I went home to my family and announced I was going to become a cowboy, they'd laugh me out of the house. My family wouldn't take my announcement seriously because I don't have the character of a cowboy. I don't like country music; I'm afraid of horseback riding; I don't like the smell of cows; and the last time I was on a farm, my allergies nearly put me in the hospital, and a goat chased me. Knowing all that...how long do you think it would take me to convince my family

I was becoming a cowboy? I'd have to prove the truth of my desire with my actions over a long period of time.

Just as I've challenged you to serve in the church, I challenge you to serve at home, too. Make your family life a priority. When you do this, you'll influence your family in great ways. There's a good chance upward influence will occur when family members see a transformation in your life. Different family members may become more motivated to change, too. I've seen this happen in homes with strained relationships. A slight attitude adjustment in the student brought peace to the home eventually. In families where parents were not Christians, I've seen these same parents come to trust Christ because of a dramatic change in their teenager's behavior. The parents wanted to investigate what caused the change in their child's life.

Changing your behavior at home is difficult because home is the one place where all your faults and failures are on display. A simple disagreement with your parents or a sibling can lead to a hurtful comment such as, "Yeah, you haven't changed at all. That church stuff doesn't work, does it? You're still immature and selfish." But life has a lot of difficulties, and perseverance is a good quality for a leader to develop. Changing your behavior at home won't be easy; you'll need to pray a lot and take the time to see change happen.

You need to understand that when you commit to be a follower of Christ and serve God as a student leader, many people will be watching how you live your life. The ones who watch most closely are in your own family. Make it a goal to be the same person at home that you are at church activities. This consistency of behavior will bring great rewards within your family over time.

Making the most of your time

Someone gave me this advice once: "If you need to get something done quickly, ask a person who is really busy to do it." I've come to understand why this advice works. Busy people are busy for a reason—they get stuff done! Busy people are the most reliable at producing results, but they can have a life out of balance because of their busyness. Unfortunately, many student leaders fit into the category of people who are overachievers and out of balance in their lives.

You need to learn as a young leader that when you say yes to something, you're saying no to something else. For example, you have lots of activities filling your schedule, and a friend asks you to try out for the school play. If you say yes to the play, you'll have to say no to other things. You have only so much time. The number of minutes in a day doesn't change to accommodate all your desires. You'll need to learn how to say no to things, or you'll overschedule yourself and have no margin in your life. When you overschedule, you'll find yourself saying no to your family, no to sleep, or no to time with God. Time with God helps you establish clear priorities about how to spend your time.

God created you intentionally with limitations. You're not designed to do everything. He made you to be dependent on others. When you decide to learn how to make the most of your time, you'll learn to say no without feeling guilty.

Just a note: Your life may not be out of balance because you're too busy. You may be out of balance because you're too self-absorbed. If you spend most of your time focusing on your own needs, you may need to take a positive step toward finding ways to get involved with helping others at home, church, and school.

Some students who are the least happy in life are the ones who are couch potatoes. They tend to be bored with life and are filled with relational tension, especially with their parents. If this describes you, you need to do something to improve your outlook on life. If you're bored, make it a goal to find something to do besides lie on the couch and watch TV or play video games. Finding constructive ways to occupy your time will help you improve your feelings about life and help you learn to be a good steward of the time God gives you.

Whether you're overstressed or underchallenged, I hope you'll take a serious look at your life and discover what you can do to bring it into balance and make the most of the time you have. You'll be amazed at what God will do with a little extra time in your schedule. Your family will notice, too, and they'll thank you for it.

when you don't agree with your parents

When you don't agree with your parents' decisions, it's best to respectfully obey what they want you to do. When children obey their parents, it's a sign of a good Christian lifestyle. The Bible says, "Children, obey your parents because you belong to the Lord, for this is the right thing to do" (Ephesians 6:1, NLT).

Obedience is one of the most powerful ways you can be an upward influence on your parents. If you pull away from your parents and rebel, you're not only disobeying God, you're also reinforcing your parents' position and opinion of you.

An incident from Hector's life is a perfect illustration of this principle. Hector was a student in our youth ministry who wanted to transfer to a different school so he could make up additional credits. He needed to make these credits up in order to graduate on time. His mom was in favor of the idea, but his dad wasn't. Wanting to honor God and respect his parents, Hector pleaded his case carefully. He didn't win. And, to his credit, he allowed their decision to stand without further argument even though he didn't agree with it. Because of Hector's obedient and positive attitude in this matter, his dad changed his mind a few days later. After speaking to both Hector and his parents, I'm convinced his dad wouldn't have changed his mind if Hector had argued, rebelled, and insisted on his way.

I can give you plenty of examples of students demanding their own way and not getting it. I'm sure you have some stories of your own. I told you Hector's story because many people don't understand this biblical principle of obedience. If you can learn it and use it, you won't always get your way, but your family life will be better. The only exception to obeying your parents is when your parents ask you to do something sinful or something against God's Word. In all other situations, your commitment to obedience will provide you with a better chance of being respected, strengthening your family, and honoring God.

communicate the essentials

Do you remember when you were a little kid and went for a ride but didn't know where you were going? You'd get strapped into a car seat by one of your parents, and you'd go along for the trip. Then every place you went people held you and passed you around the room to other people. Someone new was changing your diaper all the time. Okay, you don't remember that far back. When you're little, you can't care for yourself, and you rely on others to meet your most basic needs. But eventually, you grow up.

Unfortunately I know several students who still depend on their parents to take care of them as they did when they were toddlers. They expect their parents to know their schedules, transport them to where they need to be, fix the things they complain about, and basically meet their every need. I hope that doesn't describe you, but if it does, I'm certain this attitude causes friction between you and your parents.

Patrick, one of my former students, was this type of person. When Patrick was a senior in high school, he was surprised when his mom cried after an argument about an overdue church camp registration. The registration was late because he'd given it to his mom late, telling her to fill it out, write a check, and get it in to the church office immediately. He had a good relationship with his mom, and she'd been willing to do things for him always. As they began to discuss the situation, Patrick discovered she genuinely wanted to help him, but she was hurt he took her for granted by waiting until the last minute to give her the registration and expecting she would be able to do it.

Many families are not as healthy as this one and are not capable of talking about hurt feelings. Even within great families there is plenty of room for tension. Try to lessen your parents' pain by following some of these actions:

1. Listen to all the announcements at youth group and don't assume your parents are informed about all church activities.

2. Take extra calendars and other youth group literature home so both you and your parents have all the information.

3. Read over the calendar with your parents and discuss which programs and events you'd like to attend. Write them on the family calendar.

4. Fill out registration forms as soon as they're available and give them to your parents to sign.

5. Regularly remind your parents of your schedule and follow up on registration, transportation, and payment issues with them.

As a student leader you need to take more initiative for your life and not rely on your parents to do everything for you. You'll lower your personal stress level and strengthen your relationship with your parents. Plus, you'll prove to your parents that you're able to take on responsibility and be trusted. Many students enjoy it when they find an opportunity to help their parents trust them and give them more freedom. Better communication with your parents is one action needed to gain more trust.

Don't drain the wallet

This section could be called, "Not everything has to cost money" or "Church programs don't have to be so expensive." When the church youth ministry regularly dings your parents for money, it can put a strain on the family budget.

Money and its use is a huge issue within families and marriages. It's not uncommon for money issues to be mentioned as a key reason for a divorce. Most likely, always asking for money will not lead to a family split, but managing a family's money puts a lot of stress on a marriage relationship. In most families the subject of money is a big deal.

As a leader you can become an advocate for planning youth ministry events that are either free or inexpensive. Help your leadership team think of creative ways to lower the cost of events. Fun doesn't have to have an expensive price tag. Hanging out with other friends can be more enjoyable than a costly event. When we returned from church camp, I asked my daughter for her personal highlight of camp. She said, "Hanging out with my friends." I thought, "That's it? Not the great Bible lessons, the rock climbing, the water events, the games, the guys?" Nope! Hanging out. I'd have saved money by paying her friends to hang out at our house—that would have been cheaper than camp. Fun doesn't have to cost a lot of money.

When youth ministry events are costly, either students are left out or families make sacrifices to pay for the event. As you become more cost conscious, your youth ministry will become friendlier to families. Make sure you thank your parents regularly for their financial support. Do your part to lower the pressure on their finances by keeping costs down or helping to pay when you can.

Surprise your family...serve

When was the last time you surprised your family in a positive way? I'm sure you have examples of unpleasant surprises, but when was the last time you went out of your way to serve your family? I challenge you to look for ways to serve your family. Yep...*your family!* Leadership isn't just about serving people you're not related to. Serving with a ministry motive should include your family, too.

When you do your chores without being asked or place the needs of other family members before your own, you serve your family. When your parents have an exceptionally busy week and come home to a clean house, you've chosen an excellent way to serve them and relieve their stress. (Unless, of course—just in case my daughter reads this book—you threw away something your dad left out that he really needed!) When the lawn gets mowed, when the driveway gets swept, when you put away the laundry, when you do anything that takes a project off your parents' to-do list, you are serving them.

You may read this and say, "I do all of these things, and my parents still complain." Let me suggest that you help out before they ask you to. Then ask occasionally if there's anything you can do to help around the house. Now, you'd better know CPR just in case their hearts stop.

Earlier in this chapter I wrote about the power of upward influence. Serving your family is upward influence in action. If you do what you need to do before you're asked and do it with a positive attitude, eventually, you'll begin to have a positive influence on your family.

Family wounds are not easily or quickly healed. It takes persistent care and consistent, positive attitudes to develop a pattern of trust and changed character. If you want a healthy family, develop a servant's heart toward yours. Having a healthy family is worth the work and patience needed to take these steps. It's not easy, but it's important.

Find a model family

As I write this chapter, I'm thinking of the students who will read it and think, "I wish I had a family" or "It would be nice to feel safe at home" or "I can't relate to this; I only live with one parent and I don't feel loved." Unfortunately the reality of life is that not all teenagers grow up in a family where they experience love, support, encouragement, and safety. If that describes you, I'm deeply sorry and saddened for you. But I know there are other great families in your church from whom you can learn. Actually, it would serve you and your future marriage well to find a family to serve as a model for you. You won't find a perfect family, but look for a good one and take a lot of mental notes.

I grew up in a solid family, but I benefited from being connected to another great family. I admired the Robinsons. The mom and dad loved each other, and they were very caring to their children and their children's friends. That's where I fit in. When I was in junior high school, my best friend at church was Jimmy Robinson. His parents allowed me to be at their house, spend the night, and be part of their family gatherings. It was a great experience for me to see how another family lived and to have another family who cared for me. Even today, when I preach at my church, the Robinsons come to listen and cheer me on. It was a good thing for me to have a family, in addition to my own, where I could watch, learn, and experience the positive power of family.

As you read these words, you might know a family who serves as a model for you. If you're looking for a model family, instead of allowing it to happen spontaneously, you might want to make a more formal connection by saying something such as, "Mrs. Boyd, I just want you to know that I really look up to your family. Right now your family is serving as a model to me, and I want to thank you for allowing me to learn from your family." Not only will a comment like that serve as an encouragement to that family, but also it may make Mrs. Boyd begin to think of you differently and positively.

For example, the Cervoni kids are always in our house. If Michael Cervoni said, "Doug, I want you to know I look up to you and your family, and I'm learning a lot about marriage, parenting, and life from you and Cathy," first I would be blown away and honored. Second, I'd set my sights more clearly on Michael and look for opportunities to include him more often in our family activities.

We need models. Because family life is so important to your health and future, it would be wise to enhance your life and strengthen your leadership by finding a family you can learn from. You'll be thankful you did.

A last leadership thought and challenge

I want you to know that I realize it's very tough to be a Christian at home. It's even more difficult when you're a busy, active, and involved Christian leader. This Christian busyness results in your family receiving the worst from you and your time. Don't allow your ministry to outrank your family. You're with your family for a very short amount of time…make the most of it and honor God by honoring them.

I challenge you to write a note to your parents and thank them for something. Express your love for them and your desire to improve your relationship with them (even if it's already good). I guarantee you that your parents will save the note and consider it a treasure—they love you that much!

Alyssa's Notes

I have an incredible, strong Christian family, but this does not mean it's easy to be a student leader at home. By the time I get home, I'm tired and simply don't want to serve anymore. My mindset often is "because I am at home, I don't need to serve anymore and can instead be served." This chapter was a great reminder and wake-up call to me that I'm not being a student leader unless I'm also serving my family. When I do focus on this, I immediately realize the importance of serving my family, not just for my family's sake but also for my spiritual health.

Chapter Eight

student Leaders care about Their schools

Many school campuses are off limits to Christian influence and ministry. But while the law may limit us from talking about God on our campuses, there are no laws taking away our freedom to talk *to* God. Many are trying to keep God out of schools, but you can still connect with the heart of God while you're at school. This chapter is about connecting to our campus.

Pray for your school

I ask our student leaders to pray for their schools on a regular basis. I don't want them standing in front of the administration offices screaming prayers in an attempt to look religious. Rather I challenge them to ask God to soften their hearts for the students, teachers, and administrators at their schools. I ask them to pray for their schools' activities and for the influence of other Christians on their campuses. I want you to take on that same challenge.

I'm pleased when student leaders feel a burden for reaching the other students in their schools with the good news of God's love and God's desire for relationship with them. I don't want our students to be religious fanatics; I'm looking for students who can walk honestly through their campuses and say, "I pray for that group of students every day. I pray for the teachers and the administrators. I ask God for ways he might use me to point out his love while I'm on campus." That kind of passion for a school campus is an unbelievable testimony of God's power.

Why? Because prayer makes a difference in the lives of Christians. Prayer changes your attitude toward a teacher you don't like or a classmate who drives you crazy or an atheist who mocks your faith. Prayer changes the way people see you. When you spend time in prayer, your outward appearance reflects peace and joy that only comes from spending time with God.

See You At The Pole is an annual prayer gathering where students meet on a day in September prior to the start of the school day. They lock hands around the flagpole and pray. Each year this prayer gathering is a great opportunity for like-minded Christian students to meet and interact with each other. I encourage you to become involved with See You At The Pole at your school. But that shouldn't be the only time you pray for your school. How about praying daily for the people you meet on your campus? As you cultivate the habit of prayer, remember to include your school.

I'm not asking you to organize prayer rallies or lay hands on the school janitor or try to cast a demon out of the mascot. I want you to see your campus as a mission field. Pray for the leaders, teachers, and students at your school and for your influence on your campus. Would you like to see a God-sized revival break out on your campus? Revivals begin with dedicated believers devoted to prayer. Make a commitment to pray for your school and watch God change your heart for your school and change your school through the power of the Holy Spirit. If youth ministry student leaders aren't praying for their schools, who is?

connect with other christians

I challenge you to connect regularly with other Christians in your school. The Book of Acts tells of some benefits Christians receive from meeting together. In Acts, Christians meet each other's needs, care for each other, and worship together. Being part of a Christian community is important for a follower of Jesus.

If you don't have a solid group of Christian friends at your school, seek some out. It doesn't matter if they don't go to your church. Never bash other churches or view them as enemies. Find others who are like-minded and want to live God's way and get to know them. Meet together to encourage each other and discuss how you might work together to do something for God on your campus.

Now let me give you a word of caution about relating to your Christian friends at school: While it's essential to connect with other Christians, don't join a holy huddle that isolates you from others who aren't. The last thing your school needs is another clique—especially a Christian clique. Christian leaders need to hang out with nonbelievers so they have real-life opportunities to be the light of the world. When I've challenged student leaders to find other Christians on campus, they tell me they've discovered a lot of closet Christians. They meet students who follow Jesus personally but are not vocal or demonstrative about their faith. If you sniff these people out and meet them, you'll find amazing opportunities for connecting with one another and growing together.

You can be sure there are many other students at your school who attend church actively. Not all of those students are Christians or committed to following God's ways, but they do represent a segment of your school that could make a significant impact on your school if they came together to support each other.

Connecting with other Christians on your campus will help you with personal accountability. It's a lot easier to follow Jesus at church activities because you're surrounded by other Christians; following Jesus at school is more difficult because you're in the minority. Church events are a safe place to talk about your faith since you're in a group with people who share similar faith values; when you're on a school campus, you find yourself in the midst of very different values. And too often you tuck your faith away until the next church meeting. But it doesn't have to be that way! When others know you're a follower of Christ, you'll feel a sense of spiritual accountability to them, empowering you to live out your faith more actively on campus.

Promote school activities

Student leaders who care about their school campuses will show this by supporting school events. Don't stay hidden behind the walls of the church building. Get out and be involved with school activities and with non-Christian students. You'll model for them what a follower of Jesus looks like.

I hear constantly from school administrators, "Churches want us to support and promote their events, but they don't want anything to do with ours." Let's change that perception. Be involved in your school—remember, it's your mission field.

When you attend a school event, don't wear your Christian shirts and carry a big Bible. There's no reason to turn your appearance into a theatrical production. In Matthew 23, Jesus' harshest words are directed at people who make a show of their religion. Just go to the event and be yourself.

I watched a church youth group walk into a high school gym to watch a basketball game. They sat together, separated from everyone else. They were behaving like a holy huddle. They weren't being a light to the world. They were turning others off from knowing God. I heard another student say, "There are the snobs from First Baptist who are too good to sit with the rest of the school." Those words broke my heart. The presence of those students became a distraction from Jesus rather than a witness for him.

Being involved with a campus activity is less about promoting yourself and more about being a positive influence at your school. When you're with other students from your church at school activities, you want other students to see a group of teenagers who love being together and who care about others. Positive relationships are the best advertisements for your youth ministry. When people are attracted to your friendships, they'll be open to visiting your church. And when they visit your church, they'll hear about God and experience his love.

If it's not an immoral activity, I'd encourage you to look for ways to promote a campus event at your church. As a student leader, take the initiative and help your school by offering to advertise events. When word gets out that your church is helping to promote school activities by encouraging youth group students to attend, you'll put the church in a good light with school leaders. Simple actions help improve the relationship between the school and the church, and in today's world, that's a very positive thing.

Meet the newbies

Every school year there are great opportunities to minister to new students on your campus. I'm referring to those students who move to your school district from out of town. Any teenager who relocates into a new area is going through a major life change, and any kindness you show will be remembered.

For some the family move is a chance to start over, develop a new identity, and leave a past reputation behind. While not every new student is escaping a life of crime, each new student should be greeted and given extra attention. For most teenagers moving is a devastating experience, and leaving the familiar causes loneliness and insecurity.

When you welcome new students, they'll be thankful. Your church youth group can benefit from acts of kindness to newcomers. Don't wait for the adults to figure this out for you. You'll know about new students on your school campus before your church leaders do.

Grab a couple of friends and meet new students. Ask them questions and make sure they know you're available to help with any local contacts they may need. These helpful connections can spark friendships, be an answer to the family's prayers, and open the door for new students to be involved in your church youth group. The first few days of school are important in the beginnings of new friendships. What if you and your other church friends were the first ones to befriend a new student? You might alter the course of that person's life forever. That's an exciting idea!

As you build these new connections, make sure you invite your new friends to your youth group. Make sure someone is there to meet them and introduce them to more people. As new students to your school feel cared for by you and others in your ministry, they'll see and feel the power and the message of the gospel before they hear it.

Be clear that your motive is simply to welcome new people and not corral them as potential members of your church. Make sure your own motive is to honor God with your actions by genuinely caring for people. Don't be so aggressive in your attempts to get them to attend your youth ministry that you come off as pushy or insincere. Welcome people first; invite them to church second.

A last leadership thought and challenge

Many opportunities exist on your school campus for you to introduce God to others. But doing anything significant will be difficult if you go it alone. Find at least one other student leader and begin to pray and dream about what might happen on your campus. The student leaders at our church started Bible clubs, organized faith-based assemblies, started programs to encourage teachers, offered our church property to the school administration for events, and in many ways, became campus pastors to their schools.

If you decide to view your campus as a mission field and recognize that Jesus died for the sins of everyone there, you'll be surprised at how you begin to see your school differently. I challenge you to develop a heart for your school. Begin this development process by writing down three actions you can take at school in the next month based on what you read in this chapter. Don't try to be the most popular person on campus—just try to be the light God wants you to be.

Alyssa's Notes

I LOVE my high school. Almost anyone who knows me could tell you how often I talk about what a great school it is. But despite my great love for my school, I really don't care enough about it. Sometimes I make the excuse that I would rather focus on church ministries than campus ministries. While it might be okay to prioritize my time, it isn't okay for me to neglect my school the way I often do. And even if I don't have a large amount of time to set aside for campus ministries, I still need to pray constantly for my school. Something that has really helped me, as Doug suggests, is finding someone else to pray with me for our school.

Chapter Nine

Student Leaders Develop Other Student Leaders

I felt a call to ministry when I was in the 11th grade. The experience wasn't spooky or spiritual, and I don't really remember how I knew God wanted to use me. The call from God came while I was leading a small group of junior high boys. My youth pastor had asked me earlier to guide this group of boys who were only a few years younger than me. It was a great experience, and I use it to mark the beginning of my leadership and ministry journey. In the same way, I'd like you to set your sights on investing in the lives of others as part of your leadership journey.

Find Your Timothy

When you read the New Testament, you'll find two books named after a young leader, Timothy. The author of these books is the apostle Paul, who invested a portion of his life into leading and guiding young Timothy. Paul wrote these letters as an older adviser concerned for someone who was younger in the Christian faith and lacking in leadership experience. Mentoring is used to describe the relationship between Paul and Timothy. Paul was Timothy's mentor.

Because you've made it to the last chapter of this book, I'm assuming you've learned a lot about leadership and ministry. Now I want you to prayerfully consider finding a younger person you can advise, encourage, and mentor in leadership. You're capable of doing this for someone younger than you. I want you to become a Paul—in other words, I want you to find your own Timothy.

Paul was a great leader and mentor. His mission was to teach Timothy how to be a leader and how to overcome the obstacles Timothy might encounter in leading people older than himself. Timothy was new to ministry and inexperienced. He went through struggles common to new leaders. If you read the letters Paul sent to Timothy, you'll see the heart of a mentor who carefully coached and guided—that's what mentors do.

I hope this challenge of finding your Timothy scares you. It should...at least a little! Being a mentor is a high calling. So check your motives and make sure your heart is in the right place. Some student leaders want to become mentors so they'll have someone younger to boss around. This never works, and it's damaging to others to boost your pride and enhance your self-image in this manner. God won't reward wrong motives.

When I mentor another person, the relationship forces me to think through how to teach someone a skill I've already learned. I need to figure out how to guide him away from the kinds of mistakes I've made as a leader. The process of learning how to teach another person helps me develop new skills and teaches me how to communicate in a more mature manner. As I think and pray about how to guide the person, I learn valuable insights I can apply to my own life. And I want to live a better life. Every student I know who mentors someone younger feels the same way. Rachel sent me an e-mail that read, "When you are mentoring someone, it makes you want to live better because she is modeling her life after you, and you don't want to mess up someone's life."

Mentoring is intended to help another person learn what you have learned. If you're not growing spiritually or leading honorably, you will not be a credible or respected mentor or leader. So, to keep you on track and in the right direction, it's ideal that you have your own mentor while you're mentoring someone else.

How do you find your Timothy?

The best approach is to be available and humble. As you open yourself up to helping others, you'll begin to notice others who are seeking guidance. When you find a person you'd like to mentor, ask her if she would like to spend time with you. (Note: It's wisest for guys to mentor guys and girls to mentor girls. Motives are less confusing that way!) Maybe, to get started, you might ask for her help on a ministry project and get to know her better through serving together. Be careful not to make the person feel as if you're looking down on her or feeling superior to her. Your goal is to pass on what you've learned from other leaders and your experience to younger believers. You've been a successful mentor when the person you've mentored is able to mentor someone else eventually.

Mentoring: high calling, low attitude

When Paul mentored Timothy, he cautioned him:

> Some teachers have missed this whole point. They
> have turned away from these things and spend
> their time arguing and talking foolishness. They
> want to be known as teachers...but they don't
> know what they are talking about, even though
> they seem so confident. (1 Timothy 1:6-7, NLT)

Because you're a young leader, I want to give you a
similar warning. Don't view yourself as the *teacher*. A
good mentor recognizes he has not arrived and still has
a lot of life to figure out. You don't need an advanced
degree to mentor someone, but you do need humility.
We pursue humility because we know that if it weren't
for God's love, forgiveness, and promise of his presence
in our lives, we wouldn't have anything to offer anyone.
A humble attitude communicates that you recognize your
limitations and know you've got a lot to learn as you seek
to develop others.

If you mentor someone with an attitude of
arrogance, you'll model a negative attitude and set yourself
up for an embarrassing downfall. Humility comes from a
heart focused on God and from knowing how much he
loves you. When you focus on your inner world—your
heart—you're focusing on what's most important to God.
Jesus' harshest criticism was for the leaders of the church
who focused on the external life and not on their inner,
spiritual worlds. Jesus says—

> How terrible it will be for you teachers of religious law and you Pharisees. Hypocrites! You are like whitewashed tombs—beautiful on the outside but filled on the inside with dead people's bones and all sorts of impurity. You try to look like upright people outwardly, but inside your hearts are filled with hypocrisy and lawlessness. (Matthew 23:27-28, NLT)

As a leader committed to serving God and helping others, you'll need to give priority to your spiritual life. One of the best ways not to lose focus on God is to ask your mentor or another leader to hold you accountable. Invite that person to ask you tough questions about your heart's condition and your spiritual growth. It's easy for leaders to mix up their priorities the same way the Pharisees did... appearing healthy on the outside but being spiritually dead on the inside. Mentoring is a high calling, and it requires a humble heart.

Help others discover their gifts

Do you know that all Christians are promised spiritual gifts from God? I hope so! If not, it's time to learn about them. Some Christians don't realize God has gifted them. (You can read more about these spiritual gifts in Romans 12, 1 Corinthians 12 and 14, and Ephesians 4.) I challenge you to discover your spiritual gifts, and I dare you to play an important role in helping others discover their giftedness. If you don't know which spiritual gifts are yours, begin the journey to find out. Then help others find their gifts.

One of my favorite experiences with new Christians is to say, "Congratulations! You're gifted." I love helping people understand that God loves them enough to gift them. I hope you'll steal that phrase and use it freely with others. Model your spiritual gifts for others. Teach friends about spiritual gifts and help others identify their gifts. Once people discover their gifts and begin to use them, they develop a new excitement for their gifts and for helping others discover their spiritual gifts.

You can help others discover their gifts by complimenting them when you recognize an area of their giftedness. When you affirm a person's gifts, you inspire her to greater depths of understanding and ministry. If others are unsure of their giftedness, you can help them recognize something they don't see in themselves.

When I was in high school, my youth pastor helped me discover my giftedness. I didn't see myself as a leader or a teacher, but he did. When he began encouraging me to use these gifts, I desired to discover them. When I searched the Scriptures and learned about spiritual gifts, I realized God gave me the gift of teaching. I began to look for ways to teach others. I did this because my youth pastor, Jim, told me about God's spiritual gifts, helped me discover them, and then put me in positions to teach. As he continued to encourage me, I gradually gained more leadership experience and was given responsibilities to match these gifts.

No one has all the spiritual gifts, but every Christian has at least one spiritual gift. What gifts do you see in people in your ministry that you can affirm and develop? I challenge you to encourage the giftedness of a person in order to help develop the gift. Just as water helps grass grow, encouragement helps people develop. If people aren't encouraged, they'll never reach their potential. You'll be surprised at what happens when you offer encouragement to others.

Encourage their journey

One truth I've learned over the years is that the work of the ministry is never done. I've never heard anyone say, "I'm complete. There's nothing left for me to learn. I'm done growing spiritually." I've never heard those words because it's impossible to be perfect, complete, and lacking in nothing. There's always more for a Christian to learn, experience, and do! There are always people who need to know about Jesus. There are always more Christians who need to deepen their faith. There are more needs to be met, more programs to plan, and more worship to offer to God. There's always more!

I'll end this chapter by asking you to play a role in the encouragement of another person's spiritual growth. Everyone needs encouragement to grow. I don't know if it's happened to you, but it's easy to get discouraged with your spiritual progress. It's difficult to grow in your faith if you think you're all alone. I know so many teenagers who appreciate having another friend who cares about their faith development. I want you to be that friend and mentor to someone.

Spiritual growth can be understood best when it's described as a journey. It's a lifelong journey. Your spiritual life is moving forward, standing still, or going backward. The journey can be lonely if there's no one walking with you or cheering you on.

If you want to add a big word to your theological vocabulary, try learning the word *sanctification*. This means all Christians are in a process of being changed so they can be like Jesus. Sanctification is a process; we don't become spiritually mature immediately. But new life in Christ *is* immediate: "Therefore, if anyone is in Christ, he is a new creation; the old has gone, the new has come!" (2 Corinthians 5:17)

A maturing life is a process...a journey. I want you to be a leader who encourages others in the process of growing in Christ. Encouragement can be prayer, asking a simple question, offering a ride to church, planning an occasional meeting to talk about the faith journey... anything that gives hope to another person. Spiritual encouragement from a student leader is a powerful tool. Make encouragement part of your leadership arsenal that you pull out occasionally to lovingly nudge a friend toward greater spiritual growth.

Most Christians I know want someone to care about their lives and guide them to deeper places in their faith. And since you're taking care of your inner world and growing spiritually yourself, you'll know what others need...right?

A last leadership thought and challenge

I thank God regularly for wiring us to need each other. God doesn't want you or me to live in isolation. He created us to interact with and depend on others. God knew I couldn't be a fully devoted follower of his ways if I tried to do it alone. God knew I'd need others to play a part in my spiritual growth. I am so thankful for the many friends, mentors, and teachers who've made an impact on my life. Many of them will never know the way they've touched my life. I want you to be a leader who touches another person's life as well. You may never get recognized for it, but someday others will say your name in connection with growth in their spiritual lives. You'll have helped them become more like Jesus. Isn't that a great thing to think about?

Here's my challenge: Make a short list of people you can begin to develop intentionally. Pray for them and begin to look for ways you can influence their lives. You'll be thankful you did, and so will they.

Alyssa's Notes

Lately, God has been trying to get my attention about mentoring others. One girl asked if I would think of questions to challenge her faith so that she could grow more. Another girl directly asked if she could meet with me on a regular basis to talk about her life. While God was being quite clear that I needed to put more time and effort into mentoring others, I didn't listen until after I read this chapter (a few times). I know that life can get really busy and that mentoring can be pushed into a corner, but this chapter is a reminder to me that being a mentor is worth pursuing.

CONCLUSION - The Last Page(s)

Congratulations! Not many teenagers finish reading a book that isn't assigned to them at school. I'm very proud of you! I'd like to meet you someday and hear about what you learned through this book and what you've done with all these leadership challenges. I hope you're proud of yourself, too—reading a book that will help improve your life is a big deal.

As I wrote this book, I prayed you'd be challenged to serve God with all of your heart for the rest of your life. I hope you could tell I believe in you as a teenager. I have committed my entire adult life and ministry to helping students like you discover what happens to them when the God of the universe invades their hearts. There's nothing you can't accomplish when you tap into God's power. I sure hope that describes you!

Before writing this last page, I reread this book, and as I write these final words, I'm feeling very excited—excited to have finished writing the book and excited for you to begin putting some of these ideas into action. These nine chapters are filled with a lot of ideas and several difficult challenges designed to push you to be different from what you were when you first picked up this book and began reading.

Remember when you started reading the introduction and you wrote down your initial definition of leadership? Well, now it's time to go back to that page and write your *new* definition of leadership. Then write down some of what you learned about leadership from the book.

Don't skip the last challenge—it could be the final push you need to get going on your leadership journey. Will you share with me what you learned? I'd love to know. Please e-mail me at iamastudentleader@simplyyouthministry.com and share your new insights with me. I want to know what you plan to do with what you've learned. I will rejoice with you!

Finally, you may be finished reading, but don't throw the book away—you may need to come back and revisit these ideas as you continue your journey as a student leader! When you get discouraged, just open up the book and be reminded of God's history of using people like you and me who don't have it all together. Then think about me, an old youth pastor somewhere in California who loves teenagers just like you and is cheering for your leadership efforts. But even better than that is the fact that you've got the God of the impossible waiting to fill you, guide you, use you, change you, grow you, and mold you into a leader who loves him. Enjoy the wild ride that's waiting for you!

> Don't let anyone think less of you because you are young. Be an example to all believers in what you teach, in the way you live, in your love, your faith, and your purity. (1 Timothy 4:12, NLT)

MOVIES AND TV PROGRAMS THAT GLORIFY WITCHCRAFT AND
OCCULT PRACTICES ARE SUCKING TEENAGERS JUST LIKE YOU
INTO A WEB OF LIES. THIS BOOK DRAWS A CLEAR DISTINCTION
BETWEEN WHAT'S REAL AND WHAT'S NOT; WHAT THE BIBLE SAYS,
AND WHAT IT DOESN'T SAY WHEN IT COMES TO THE
SUPERNATURAL.

Don't Buy the Lie
Discerning Truth in a World of Deception
Mark Matlock

RETAIL $9.99
ISBN 0-310-25814-6

WHEN YOU THINK OF JESUS' DISCIPLES, YOU NEVER THINK
OF THEM AS A BUNCH OF CLUELESS, FEARFUL, IMMATURE,
DISCOURAGED GUYS—DO YOU? NO, YOU THINK OF THEM AS
BOLD AND COMMITTED. BUT THE TRUTH IS THAT EVEN
JESUS' CLOSEST FRIENDS WENT THROUGH TIMES OF
LONELINESS, DOUBT, AND CONFUSION. SOMETIMES
FOLLOWING GOD IS TOUGH. LEARN HOW TO STICK TO IT
THROUGH THE GOOD AND BAD WITH THIS 30-DAY JOURNAL.

Devotion
A Raw-Truth Journal on Following Jesus

Mike Yaconelli

RETAIL $10.99
ISBN 0-310-25559-7

invert

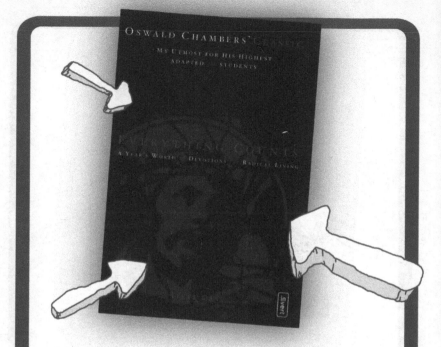

THE CLASSIC OSWALD CHAMBERS' *MY UTMOST FOR HIS HIGHEST* ADAPTED FOR STUDENTS, THIS DAILY DEVOTIONAL DUMPS THE PLEASANTRIES OF RELIGION AND LEADS YOUR STUDENTS TO REAL FAITH. EACH DAY INCLUDES A SCRIPTURE REFERENCE, AN EXCERPT FROM THE CLASSIC TEXT, AND A PHRASE STUDENTS CAN EASILY MEMORIZE TO REMIND THEM ABOUT THE REALITY OF BEING A CHILD OF GOD.

Everything Counts
A Year's Worth of Devotions on Radical Living

Steven Case

RETAIL $14.99
ISBN 0-310-25408-6